First World War
and Army of Occupation
War Diary
France, Belgium and Germany

38 DIVISION
113 Infantry Brigade,
Brigade Machine Gun Company
17 May 1916 - 27 February 1918

WO95/2556/3

The Naval & Military Press Ltd
www.nmarchive.com
Published in association with The National Archives

Published by

The Naval & Military Press Ltd

Unit 10 Ridgewood Industrial Park,

Uckfield, East Sussex,

TN22 5QE England

Tel: +44 (0) 1825 749494

www.naval-military-press.com

www.nmarchive.com

This diary has been reprinted in facsimile from the original. Any imperfections are inevitably reproduced and the quality may fall short of modern type and cartographic standards.

© **Crown Copyright**
Images reproduced by permission of The National Archives, London, England, 2015.

Contents

Document type	Place/Title	Date From	Date To
Heading	WO95/2556/3		
Heading	113th Machine Gun Coy. May 1916-Feb 1918		
Heading	113 M G Coy Vol I		
War Diary	Le Havre	17/05/1916	17/05/1916
War Diary	Rest Camp I	18/05/1916	18/05/1916
War Diary	Les Puresbecques	19/05/1916	24/05/1916
War Diary	On Road	25/05/1916	25/05/1916
War Diary	Le Drumez	26/05/1916	11/06/1916
War Diary	Les Puresbecques	12/06/1916	12/06/1916
War Diary	Cense La Vallee	13/06/1916	13/06/1916
War Diary	Cauchy-A-La-Tour	15/06/1916	15/06/1916
War Diary	La Ferme	16/06/1916	26/06/1916
War Diary	Boffles	27/06/1916	27/06/1916
War Diary	Bernaville	28/06/1916	30/06/1916
Heading	113th Machine Gun Company. July 1916		
Heading	War Diary For July 1916 113 M.G. Coy.		
War Diary	Herissart	01/07/1916	01/07/1916
War Diary	Lealvillers	02/07/1916	03/07/1916
War Diary	Treux	04/07/1916	05/07/1916
War Diary	Mametz	06/07/1916	11/07/1916
War Diary	Treux	12/07/1916	12/07/1916
War Diary	On The Road	13/07/1916	13/07/1916
War Diary	Ailly	14/07/1916	14/07/1916
War Diary	Brucamps	15/07/1916	15/07/1916
War Diary	Authie	16/07/1916	17/07/1916
War Diary	Couin	18/07/1916	20/07/1916
War Diary	Bivouac Couin	20/07/1916	23/07/1916
War Diary	Mailly Maillet	24/07/1916	28/07/1916
War Diary	Bus Aux Bois	29/07/1916	30/07/1916
War Diary	On The Road	31/07/1916	31/07/1916
Heading	113 Machine Gun Coy. War Diary For August 1916 Vol 4		
War Diary	La Grange Rouge	01/08/1916	01/08/1916
War Diary	Jan Ter Biezen	02/08/1916	17/08/1916
War Diary	Ypres Salient	20/08/1916	31/08/1916
Heading	War Diary 113th Machine Gun Company For September 1916		
War Diary	Ypres Salient	01/09/1916	07/09/1916
War Diary	A. 23.c. 1 1/2. 7	08/09/1916	17/09/1916
War Diary	The Salient	18/09/1916	19/09/1916
War Diary	Ypres Salient	20/09/1916	30/09/1916
Heading	War Diary 113 Machine Gun Coy. October 1916		
War Diary	Ypres Salient	01/10/1916	15/10/1916
War Diary	A. 22.d.8.3	16/10/1916	24/10/1916
War Diary	Rest Camp A.22.d.8.3	25/10/1916	25/10/1916
War Diary	Ypres Salient	26/10/1916	31/10/1916
Heading	War Diary For November 1916 113 Machine Gun Company.		
War Diary	Ypres Salient (Left Sector) Of Left Inf. Bde. Ref. St Julien 28 N.W.	01/11/1916	03/11/1916

War Diary	Ypres Salient Ref. St. Julien 28 N.W.	04/11/1916	15/11/1916
War Diary	Ref. Belgium 28.N.W. Ed 3D "S" Camp. A 22d.9.3	16/11/1916	16/11/1916
War Diary	'S' Camp	17/11/1916	25/11/1916
War Diary	Canal Bank	26/11/1916	30/11/1916
Heading	113th Machine Gun Coy. War Diary For December 1916		
War Diary		01/12/1916	31/12/1916
Heading	War Diary For January 1917 113 Machine Gun Company. Vol 9		
War Diary	Ypres Sector	01/01/1917	28/02/1917
Heading	113th Machine Gun Company. War Diary For March 1917		
War Diary	Ypres Sector	01/03/1917	31/03/1917
Heading	113 Machine Gun Company. War Diary For April 1917		
War Diary	Ypres Sector	01/04/1917	31/05/1917
Heading	113th Machine Gun Company War Diary For June 1917		
War Diary	In The Line	11/06/1917	13/06/1917
War Diary	Ypres Salient	14/06/1917	30/06/1917
Heading	113 Machine Gun Company. War Diary July-1917		
War Diary	Ypres	01/07/1917	31/07/1917
Heading	113 Machine Gun Company. War Diary August-1917		
War Diary	Pilckem Iron Cross Ridge	01/08/1917	30/08/1917
Miscellaneous	Operation During Period 31 July To 4 August 1917	18/08/1917	18/08/1917
Heading	113th Machine Gun Company War Diary For September 1917		
War Diary	Ypres Salient (Malakoff Fm)	01/09/1917	09/09/1917
War Diary	Proven 2H 9.7 Hazenbrouk Camp	09/09/1917	16/09/1917
War Diary	H 3 & H4 Belgium & Part Of Proven Sheet 36	17/09/1917	30/09/1917
Heading	113th Machine Gun Company War Diary For October 1917		
War Diary	Bois Grenier Section	01/10/1917	31/10/1917
Heading	113 Machine Gun Company. War Diary For November 1917 Vol 19		
War Diary	Bois Grenier Sector	01/11/1917	29/11/1917
Heading	113th Machine Gun Company War Diary For December 1917 Vol 20		
War Diary	Bois Grenier Sector (Sheet 36NW France Belgium Map Sheet 36 Radinghem Reference Maps)	01/12/1917	23/12/1917
War Diary	Bois Grenier & Fleurbaix		
Heading	113th Machine Gun Company War Diary For January 1918		
War Diary	Heurbaix	01/01/1918	13/01/1918
War Diary	Bac St Maur	14/01/1918	31/01/1918
Heading	War Diary 113 Machine Gun Company February 1918 Vol 22		
War Diary	Enguinegatte	01/02/1918	11/02/1918
War Diary	Guarbenrie	12/02/1918	12/02/1918
War Diary	Neuf Berquin.	13/02/1918	13/02/1918
War Diary	Armentieres	14/02/1918	27/02/1918

HOQS/3556/3

38TH DIVISION
113TH INFY BDE

113TH MACHINE GUN COY.

MAY 1916 - FEB 1918

113 MG Cag Vol 1

Army Form C. 2118

WAR DIARY or INTELLIGENCE SUMMARY

(Erase heading not required.)

113 M.G. Coy. for May 17 to 31st 1916

Vol 1

Instructions regarding War Diaries and Intelligence Summaries are contained in F.S. Regs., Part II. and the Staff Manual respectively. Title Pages will be prepared in manuscript.

Place	Date	Hour	Summary of Events and Information	Remarks and references to Appendices
LE HAVRE	17	13.30	Arrived by boat intact	
Rest Camp I	18	14.0	Left for Les Puresbecques at 14.0. Arrival intact	
Les Puresbecques	19	—		
"	20	—		
"	21	—	1 sick to Hospital	
"	22	20.30	Effects of Lachrymose shell fell at 20.30 - 21.30	
"	23	—	1 sick to Hospital	
"	24	—	The bare minimum for running the company was added on arrival at Billets by 22 men from the R.W.F.	
On Road	25	—	1 sick to Hospital. Winchester shelled: about six shrapnel. No. 3 emplacement fired 200 rounds	
LE DRUMEZ	26	—	1 sick to Hospital. Winchester shelled. New enemy M.G. emplacement suspected at M36.C.2.6. Fired at from M35.2	
"	27	15.30	WINCHESTER & ERITH shelled. New emplacement ERITH shelled; 30 or 40 H.E. at 15.30. No damage. 500 rounds fired on hostile working party from No.2 emp.ment. SURPRISE occupied. Wires down in two places.	
"	28	—	New post DARTFORD occupied.	
"	29	—	Gun at ERITH pinched by bullets through exploded left loophole: Gun useless. Light overhead emplacement commenced new WINCHESTER. Hamlet MEURIN near RUE DU HEM shelled from 14.20 to 14.45 & 16.30 to 16.40. Two houses burned.	Stood to 21.12 from H.A.
"	30	—	Heavy bombardment from 19.0 to 21.30. No MG's damaged. Loophole on left of ERITH filled in. Reserve ammunition stores built in all Posts & emplacements. Stand to at 21.12	
"	31	—	Bombing attack by our infantry. R.W.F. Kept M.G. quiet at 30.C.2.2 until 24.30 when M.G. fired 300 rounds at hostile M.G. emplacement.	Signed E.H.W.

No 113 MACHINE GUN COY.
1 JUN 1916

WAR DIARY
or
INTELLIGENCE SUMMARY
(Erase heading not required.)

Army Form C. 2118.

Place	Date	Hour	Summary of Events and Information	Remarks and references to Appendices
LE DRUMEZ	1		Two hundred emplacements constructed. One man hit in thigh off helmet of another. Shell from hostile anti-aircraft fell in our lines marked G.F. 13 P.R. — W.I.P. — F.S. or Co. — 24.7.15	
"	2	6 P.M.	Indirect night firing commenced. 2500 rounds expended.	
"	3		Quiet day. Our trench mortars at work. 2500 rounds expended.	
"	4		Trench mortars bombarded enemy line & a successful raid carried out. 7250 rounds expended by our M.G. Indirect	
"	5		Fired 370 from front line on hostile working party. Indirect 4500 rounds. One man lightly wounded in listening party.	
"	6		Two men to hospital sick. Three men added to strength from Base. Indirect fire 4,000.	
"	7		Indirect 3,900 fired. Draw trench dug by R.W.T.	
"	8		Sergeant wounded in head inside MOATED GRANGE, no helmet on. 750 rounds at hostile M.G. pilound it. 4000 Indirect	
"	9		Three to hospital sick. Quiet day. Sergt A. Michie acquitted at F.G.C.M. under Sec. 9.2. 3500 Indirect	
"	10		700 fired at hostile wiring party & dispersed it. 3500 Indirect. One to hospital sick. at 6 A.M. two of our shells fell & burst within 100 x of LONELY.	
"	11		Two to hospital sick. Very quiet day. Relieved at 6:30 to 10:30 P.M. by 116 M.G. Coy. marched to LES PUISBELGOES last section arriving 4 A.M.	
LES PUISBELGOES CENSE LA VALLEE	12		Left at 11:30 A.M. arrived CENSE LA VALLEE 5:30 P.M. Room full out.	
COMTE " "	13		Rest few whole day. Good billets. rained all day.	
CAVCHY-A-LA-TOUR	14		Left COMTE at 12:15 P.M. joined the 118 Bgd. & passed through AVCHEL on to CAVCHY-A-LA-TOUR where Division was billeted. Then advanced one hour to 11 P.M. Room full out.	
"	15		Left at 6:45 A.M. joined column at FLORIN GHAM. marched through PERNES to BAILLEOL-AUX-CORNAILES & on to our	
LA FERME	16		Billet at LA FERME DU BOIS DE LA MOTTE, where we arrived at 12:30 P.M. Room full out. Three sent to Base for further training. Cold weather.	

Army Form C. 2118.

Vol 2 June

WAR DIARY
or
INTELLIGENCE SUMMARY
(Erase heading not required.)

XXXVIII

No. 113 MACHINE GUN COY.
30 JUN 1916
MACHINE GUN CORPS

Place	Date	Hour	Summary of Events and Information	Remarks and references to Appendices
LAFERME	17		One sick returned from hospital. Two added to the strength. Gun drill & cleaning fatigues. Nine north aeroplanes passed over	
"	18		One to hospital sick. N.E. wind & cold. L/Cpl. A. Dick sentenced 90 days F.P. No 1. 60 days remitted on Sec. F.2. Inspection by General M. de la Hill. Guns painted for invisibility	
"	19		Attack training 6.30 to 1.30. Rain & cold	
"	20		One sick to hospital. Attack training with view to supply of ammunition.	
"	21		Attack training 8.30 to 1.30	
"	22		One to Base for further instruction. Two from Base added to strength. 5 A.M. to 9 A.M. Range shooting. Hostile planes bombed St. Pol. Very hot day.	
"	23		One sick to hospital. One returned from hospital. Hot day & stormy. Attack training with Bn. T.W.F.	
"	24		One sick to hospital. Divisional attack & consolidation training. Heavy rain. Heavy sunfire heard.	
"	25		Divisional training for attack. Lived on Iron rations. Aeroplane passed over at night dropping lights.	
"	26		Two to hospital sick. Left Billets at 4.30 P.M. marched through Ligny St. Flochel, Vacquerie Le Moocp to BOFFLES where arrived at 3.A.M 27.6.16. Rain heavy the whole march. Tents faint led. No one fell out.	
BOFFLES	27		Left at 6.30 P.M. joined H.Q. staff & marched via Villiers L'Hopital, Le Meillard to BERNAVILLE where arrived at 1 A.M. fine night. No one fell out. # One from hospital	
BERNAVILLE	28		Rain all morning. Further tents postponed 48 hours. Four men to hospital	
"	29		Three from hospital. Seven men from Base posted to the company	
"	30		Preparation for move to HERISSART	

2449 Wt. W14957/Mgo 750,000 1/16 J.B.C. & A. Forms/C.2118/12.

B.H. Bodman Capt.
O.C. 113 Coy M.G. Corps

113th Inf.Bde.
38th Div.

WAR DIARY

113th MACHINE GUN COMPANY.

J U L Y

1 9 1 6

WAR DIARY FOR JULY 1916

113 M.G. Coy.

Vol 3

INTELLIGENCE SUMMARY

(Erase heading not required.)

Instructions regarding War Diaries and Intelligence Summaries are contained in F.S. Regs., Part II. and the Staff Manual respectively. Title Pages will be prepared in manuscript.

Place	Date	Hour	Summary of Events and Information	Remarks and references to Appendices
HÉBUTERNE	July 1.	7.30 AM	Franco-British attack begun. Our company move to LEALVILLERS at 9.30 P.M.	
LEALVILLERS	2		Prepared guns for firing.	
"	3	9.? P.M.	Moved by road to TREUX via VARENNES, SENLIS. Heavy rain.	
TREUX	4	12 P.M.	Thunderstorm.	
"	5	12.0 P.M.	Orders to move up in fighting order. Some officers moved forward with H.Q. staff of Bgd. 113 Coy. entered trenches by road S.W. of MAMETZ with all limbers stopping short of village of MAMETZ. Coy. in trenches, 5 guns in WHITE TRENCH. 26692 Pte Elcock wounded shrapnel. 5 M.G. emplacements built in WHITE TRENCH. Trench heavily bombarded.	
MAMETZ	6		Heavy rain all day. Both artillery active. 2nd Lieut. Niven J. wounded (shell shock) 16218 27445 Pte Burns W, 27446 Pte Bingham R, 26959 Pte Little W, 21708 Pte Thomas (R.W.F.) 16218 L/Cpl. Williams (R.W.F) all shrapnel wounds. Infantry on our left at 8 A.M. attacked left of MAMETZ wood. assisted by 3 M.Guns – 3900 rounds fired. From 8.30 A.M. to 3 P.M. enemy bombarded WHITE TRENCH, guns dismounted & emplacements were smashed by hostile shelling. Four guns sent up to Bunny Trench.	
"	7		Occasional light showers. Heavy bombardment of line at 6 P.M. Aeroplanes active. Five guns relieved in WHITE TRENCH, trench heavily shelled, one gun frame & vessels in trench behind knocked out.	
"	8		2 guns put in CLIFF TRENCH to fire overhead at night on to STRIP TRENCH. 11874 Pte Dice #A. 11265 Pte Gallacher J, 31025 Pte Barraclough J. all sick to hospital. The following killed in the wood. 2nd Lieut. Tanner E.J.S., 21560 Pte Rogers J.B. (R.W.F.) 16592 Pte Tyler H. (R.W.F) 26686 Pte Bright H., 26708 Cpl. Watts R., 26710 L/Cpl. Beard H., 26931 Hall C. 20 men attached from R.W.F. 113 Bgd.	

INTELLIGENCE SUMMARY

(Erase heading not required.)

Instructions regarding War Diaries and Intelligence Summaries are contained in F.S. Regs, Part II. and the Staff Manual respectively. Title Pages will be prepared in manuscript.

Place	Date	Hour	Summary of Events and Information	Remarks and references to Appendices
MAMETZ	9		Bombardment continued all day & night.	
"	10	4.15 AM	38th Div. attacks MAMETZ WOOD & makes good progress; part of attack held up at SUNKEN ROAD for about one hour; 4 guns & one officer advance with 3rd line of 16 R.W.F. & take up covering positions in SUNKEN ROAD & fired on enemy. Hostile M.G. was silenced & enemy recently killed. Gunners were seen afterwards with bullet wounds. Four more guns sent up in advance to fringe of the wood – with temporary loss of 8 guns owing to both Nos. 2 being wounded. Two more guns taken to x roads 350x into the wood, stayed two hours & swept their front. These guns were again taken further up about 100x along CENTRAL DRIVE; these guns were put in position ready for action & stayed till noon, then advanced again with infantry another ½ mile meeting with no resistance. One of these two guns was later put out of action by a bullet piercing the barrel casing. Leaving off the barrel & making its exit at the rear of barrel casing. Remaining gun with infantry withdrew 300x to allow our artillery to shell the wood. 2nd Lieut. CULLEN & 2 in CENTRAL DRIVE 250x beyond Railway Crossing, 2 more with 2.Lt. CULLEN entrenched to 15 R.W.F. & 2nd Lt. ODGERS took 4 guns to 13 R.W.F. on the left. 26966 Pte Campbell W. killed. The following were wounded.... 14054 Sergt. Daniels, 23391 Pte James T. (R.W.F.) 18866 Pte Jones J. (R.W.F) 20637 Pte Hughes A. (R.W.F.) 25836 Pte Horton W. 26978 Pte Smith J., 26973 Pte Waring H., 26969 Pte Donnelly S., 27693 Sergt. Michie A (shot through 6th insc.), 11861 Pte Byres A. 11859 Pte Davies J., 11866 Pte Kennedy I., 10709 Pte Riley T (R.W.F.) sick to hospital. Coy. withdrew to MINDEN POST & rested. Left MINDEN POST at 6 P.M. & marched to TREUX arriving at 10 P.M.	
"	11		2nd Lieut. CULLEN was cut off for some time with his gun, the rest of his guns remained up in line when the infantry retired too much. On the infantry returning it is possible they mistook CULLEN in his isolated position for an enemy, but there is no doubt he was shot by our own men.	

INTELLIGENCE SUMMARY

(Erase heading not required.)

Instructions regarding War Diaries and Intelligence Summaries are contained in F.S. Regs., Part II. and the Staff Manual respectively. Title Pages will be prepared in manuscript.

3

Place	Date	Hour	Summary of Events and Information	Remarks and references to Appendices
MAMETZ	11		The following were killed in action:— 2nd Lieut. CULLEN W.H., 28078 Sergt. JOHNSON E., 11863 Pte BATH GATE S., 16322 Pte WILLIAMS S.(R.W.F.). The following are missing:— 6181 Pte WATKINS B., 22027 Pte VARNALS A.W. (R.W.F.), 19533 Pte DAVIDSON W (R.W.F.), 27626 L/Cpl. KNIGHT W (R.W.F.), 22919 Pte STANLEY L. (R.W.F.), 22305 Pte MALGER G. (R.W.F.), 20376 Pte MORGAN E. (R.W.F.), 21981 Pte FRENCH E. (R.W.F.), 22194 Pte REARDON D. (R.W.F.). The following reported missing now officially reported in hospital, his wound. 6488 Pte GLENTON W. (R.W.F.)	
TREUX	12		Left TREUX at 6 A.M. arrived RIBEMONT station to entrain at 7.10 A.M. Arrangements so bad that we did not leave the station until 9 P.M. & arrived at LONGPRE at 1.40 A.M. tea supplied by Y.M.C.A. Div. General Von Phirpe Salt sent to England.	
In the road	13		Left LONGPRE at 2.15 A.M. marched to AILLY LE HAUT CLOCHER, arriving at 5.45 A.M. Billeted.	
AILLY	14		Left AILLY marched to BRUCAMPS most comfortably billeted. Channel Sims for first time, having wool as transport did not so with us: Lavrils were very badly fouled & one spoiled.	
BRUCAMPS	15		Left BRUCAMPS at 8 A.M. by motor buses & arrival at AUTHIE at 2 P.M. very dirty billets. General cleaning up of ammunition etc.	
AUTHIE	16			
	17		Left AUTHIE, marched to COUIN about 4 miles & were in bivouac in woods. Rain all day.	
COUIN	18		Left COUIN at 9.30 P.M. Q. marched to bivouac by COIGNEAUX stayed the night. 2 men to hospital sick. One Sergt. from Trench reinforcement.	
	19		Moved bivouac at 11.30 A.M. back a mile. Wind N.W. & fine. 6 to hospital sick, 1 to hospital sick from hospital.	
	20		Hot & fine. N. wind. Gun & belt cleaning. 6 to hospital sick, 1 from hospital.	

R.H. Bosham Capt
& 11th n.f.

INTELLIGENCE SUMMARY

(Erase heading not required.)

Instructions regarding War Diaries and Intelligence Summaries are contained in F.S. Regs., Part II. and the Staff Manual respectively. Title Pages will be prepared in manuscript.

Place	Date	Hour	Summary of Events and Information	Remarks and references to Appendices
Bivouac Colin	20		Captain BADHAM T.H. left us to take up duties as 2nd i/c of 1/4 R.W.F. & 2nd Lieut ODGERS S.E. appointed as O.C. 113 Coy. M.G.C. Heavy gun fire all night.	
" "	21		2 to hospital sick. Fine & warm N. wind. 1 one officer & 50 O.R. on working party at 12.45 P.M. another officer & 25 O.R. on working party at 6.45 P.M.	
" "	22		Fine day. Working party to BLACKFRIARS 6.30 to 10.30 A.M. one N.C.O. & 15 O.R.	
			" " P.M. to 5 P.M. " 1 " & 20 "	
			" " No. 4 Strong Point at 8 P.M. 1 officer & 20 "	
			" " 12 noon to 9 P.M. 1 " & 20 " (one man wounded)	
			18176 JONES D. wounded (R.W.F.) 16843 BROCK J. returned to BASE under age; 46201 THOMAS W.J. R.A.M.C. transferred for water duties. 2 O.R. to hospital.	
" "	23		Cooler N. wind. Two parties under N.C.O. for loading. One officer & 40 O.R. wiring at No. 4 Strong Point from 9 P.M. to 3.15 A.M. One to hospital & one from hospital.	
Mailly Maillet	24		Moved from bivouac at 10 A.M. & marched to MAILLY MAILLET arriving at 12.30 P.M.; arrived the 36 Coy. M.G.C. at 12.30; right section in trenches, 4 in first line defences, 4 in 2nd line of defence. Reliefs complete at 4.30 P.M. Draft as reinforcements 4 Sergts. 31 O.R. 2 O.R. to hospital sick	
" "	25		Fine, hot. Enemy heavily shelled guns at K.33.c.y.7. Wind N.W. Gun emplacements improved. 3 new officers arrived. 2 O.R. to hospital sick	
" "	26		Fine. Artillery action on both sides. Village shelled at 9.30 P.M. New gun emplacement built at K.28.d.2.1; gun have fired 1750 rounds overhead at night. Communicating trench to SACKVILLE STREET deepened. Open emplacement at VIEW TRENCH strengthened. 3 O.R. discharged from hospital.	

B.R.DuBois
113 M.G.C.

INTELLIGENCE SUMMARY

(Erase heading not required.)

Instructions regarding War Diaries and Intelligence Summaries are contained in F.S. Regs., Part II. and the Staff Manual respectively. Title Pages will be prepared in manuscript.

Place	Date	Hour	Summary of Events and Information	Remarks and references to Appendices
Mailly Maillet Bos aux Bois	27		Fine day. Light rain in early morning. Sixteen concertinas built in billets & sent up to the line.	
"	28		61st M.G. Coy. relieved us by 4.45 P.M. & we marched to Bos aux Bois where we took over bivouac.	
Bos aux Bois	29		Bus was evacuated at 6.45 A.M. & we marched to THIEVRES where we were well billeted. Hot weather. 2 O.R. discharged from hospital.	
"	30		Sunday. Very hot. Coy. marched by sections to DOULENS via ORVILLE & AMPLIER. Each section & limbers was entrained with a Battalion of the K.W.F. First sect. left station at 18.19. 2nd Sec. at 21.19. 3rd Sec. at 0.19. 4th Sec. at 3.19. (31-7-16) Motors & limbers were entrained in two minutes leaving us over two hours rest in station.	
On the Road	31		Arrived at HOPOUTRE at 9 A.M., detrained & marched to a farm called LA GRANGE ROUGE just off the ~~Ypres~~ YPRES Road via ABEELE, WATOU & on road to WUMEZEELE. Army hot day. Four men fell out from the Company.	

B.T. Dribos Lt.
118 M.G.C.

Vol 4

113 Machine Gun Coy

War Diary for August 1916.

WAR DIARY
or
INTELLIGENCE SUMMARY
(Erase heading not required.)

Army Form C. 2118

August 1916

Place	Date	Hour	Summary of Events and Information	Remarks and references to Appendices
La Grange Rouge	1		Hot weather. Two men from Hospital.	
Jan Ter Biezen	2		Moved from billet by road to Jan Ter Biezen via Houtkerque.	
"	3		Hot. Nine men arrived as draft from Base. One man to Base under esc. One to Hospital sick.	
"	4		Routine. Mostly tactical exercises.	
"	5		" Two O.R. from Hospital.	
"	6			
"	7		One sick to Hospital.	
"	8		Hot. Wind Easterly. Heavy bombardment heard. Gas felt strongly at 10.30 P.M. Ordered to stand to at 10.58	
"	9		Stood down at 12.55 A.M. Horses slightly affected by gas.	
"	10		Hot. One sick to Hospital. One from hospital.	
"	11		Teams ran 300x set into action on a target in 1.35" as practice. Ten men attached from R.W.F. to complete. 32 attached for training etc. Three O.R. from Base.	
"	12		Training in Wood fighting	
"	13		Stiff West wind	
"	14 } 15 } 16 }		Routine	
"	17		Showery	
"	18		Fine. Received orders to move to Ypres Salient.	
"	19		Heavy rain. 2nd Lieut. S. E. Odgers joins 61 M.G.C. as 2nd i/c. Col. B. H. Tsadram returns as C.O.	

B. R. Dulles Lt.
2nd i/c for O.C. 113 M.G.C.

Army Form C. 2118

WAR DIARY or INTELLIGENCE SUMMARY
(Erase heading not required.)

Instructions regarding War Diaries and Intelligence Summaries are contained in F.S. Regs., Part II. and the Staff Manual respectively. Title Pages will be prepared in manuscript.

Place	Date	Hour	Summary of Events and Information	Remarks and references to Appendices
YPRES SALIENT	20		Showery. Left bivouac at 7.30 P.M. marched to POPERINGHE, entrained at 9.25 P.M., detrained at Level crossing, marched to Ypres where some shells fell, then on to our H.Q. at C.19.c.3.6 on West bank of CANAL arriving at 11 P.M. Took over from 10th Bgl. M.G.C. & completed reliefs by 3.30 A.M. Gun positions held at various points in Support lines & three in front line. Reserve men left at ELVERDINGHE & Transport at A.23.c.4.9. Wind just WEST OF NORTH. Gas alert on.	
	21		Gas warning sounded & helmets put on for 20 minutes. Gas warning again at 6 P.M. & respirators taken off again in half an hour. Wind 10 M.P.H.	
	22		GAS ALERT on all day. Wind in the NORTH.	
	23		Fine. Wind W.	
	24 25 26		Fine. West wind. Improving existing Emplacements. One sick to hospital.	
	27 28		One sick to hospital	
	29		Wind backing to S.E. Rain all day. Thunderstorm in afternoon. Gas Alert on. Gas attack alarms sounded at 11 P.M. Helmets worn. No gas here.	
	30		GAS ALERT off. Strong wind + heavy rain. Many Dugouts on banks of YPERLEE crumbling down, owing to rain. Indirect fire at night. 500 rounds fired from C.19.c.2.3 on to part of GERMAN line running Northward from C.7.a.3.1 just point 83. One sick to hospital. One returned from Base.	
	31		Fine day. Wind N.W. Aeroplane activity. Overhead fire 500 as yesterday.	

B. T. Dilkes Lt.
acting for O.C. 113 M.G.C.

1875 Wt. W593/826 1,000,000 4/15 T.R.C.&A. A.D.S.S./Forms/C. 2118.

WAR DIARY
113th. MACHINE GUN COMPANY
FOR SEPTEMBER 1916

Vol 5

WAR DIARY or **INTELLIGENCE SUMMARY**

Army Form C. 2118.

No. 113 MACHINE GUN COY. 1 OCT 1916 MACHINE GUN CORPS.

Place	Date	Hour	Summary of Events and Information	Remarks and references to Appendices
YPRES SALIENT	1		Showery. Wind West. Heavy bombardment by both sides. Reports that enemy possibly preparing for raid. Special orders issued to Guns at C.14.C.9.1. Night passed quietly. Overhead from C.19.a.2.3 to FARM 14. 1000 rounds fired.	
"	2		Certain amount of hostile shelling. Hostile M.G. silenced by indirect fire from C.19.a.2.3. Wind S.E. GAS ALERT ON. Three Gas alarms, 11.30 P.M. 1.50 A.M. & 2.55 A.M. of 3.9.16. 500 rounds fired.	
"	3		Wind N.W. Fine & cool. C.14.C.9.1 shelled, no damage.	
"	4		Orders received for Bgde. relief. Hostile M.G. located C.14.a.2.6. Gas alert received 12.15 A.M. from front line. Wind N.N.W. Considerable hostile M.G. fire over FARGATE.	
"	5		Rainy day. 1 O.R. from hospital.	
"	6		Gas alert on. Shell landed on M.G. dugout at C.14.C.9.1 without detonating. Hostile T.M⁵ & M.G⁵ very active. One O.R. from hospital sick One man to England on special pass.	
"	7		All guns relieved by 115 M.G. Coy. by 3.30 A.M. marched by sections to rest camp arriving 4.50 A.M.	
A.23.C.1¼.7	8		Very fine. Seven men transferred from R.W.F. to the Company. Two men from hospital.	
	9		Fine day. Routine & tactical M.G. work.	

B.H.Commons

WAR DIARY or INTELLIGENCE SUMMARY

Army Form C. 2118.

Place	Date	Hour	Summary of Events and Information	Remarks and references to Appendices
A.23.c.14.7	10		Cooler. Wind N.E. Fatigues collecting rubble.	
"	11		Sent six men to BASE ETAPLES, to join Infantry, unfitted for M.Gun work.	
"	12		Fine. N.W. wind. Gas alert off. New small box respirators issued & tested. Range practice. Revolver practice. Captain B.H. BADHAM, gazetted Major (Temp) as from 14.7.16. 800 rounds fired.	
"	13		North wind, cooler. 1050 rounds fired on Range. Revolver range practice. 2nd Lt. F.H. CHAMPION goes on leave.	
"	14		North wind stress. Heavy showers. Leave started. [crossed out]	
"	15		Wind North. Heavy showers at night. Tanks used on SOMME.	
"	16		Wind N.W. Fine. Two men to Hospital sick.	
"	17		Fine. Left camp at 6 P.M. marched via BRIELEN & VLAMERTINGHE, arrived CANAL BANK 9.45 P.M. Relief complete at 1.15 A.M.	
The SALIENT	18		Wind W. by S. Rain all day. Trenches falling in. Built too night firing emplacements one at C.13.c.3.8 & one at C.19.a.2.3. 1000 rounds fired. One sick to hospital.	
"	19		Rain in the morning. Overhead fire at night. 1500 rounds. Thunder at 2 P.M. Gas alert on. Signaller R.J. SHOULDER given Military Medal for an act of gallantry. Keeping the wires mended at MAMETZ July 6 to July 11 under continuous shell fire. R.J. Shoulder went on leave. One to hospital sick.	

WAR DIARY or INTELLIGENCE SUMMARY

Army Form C. 2118.

No. 113 MACHINE GUN COY.
1 OCT 1916
MACHINE GUN CORPS

Place	Date	Hour	Summary of Events and Information	Remarks and references to Appendices
Ypres Salient	20		Gas alert off. Wind N.N.W. Rain most of day. Bombing raid by R.W.F. unsuccessful. Overhead fire 500 rounds. One man from hospital. Pt. Herod J. returns from England.	
"	21		Gas alert on: showery. Working parties on night firing emplacements shelled. Hostile O.B. up. One man to hospital sick.	
"	22		Very fine. Wind East. Two prisoners brought in from hostile patrol, who lost their way in our wire. Poperinghe shelled.	
"	23		Very fine & warm. Wind S.E. Overhead fire at night 1500 rounds from C.19.a.2.3 on to R.N.S.O.4.8.9.7.31 C.7.a.3.7. One to hospital sick.	
"	24		Very fine. Wind S. Guns at C.19.a.14.2½ night firing onto C.7.C.1.9 - C.7.a.3.7. Guns at C.19.a.3.6 fired on to X-roads at C.3.a.8.7. 3100 rounds. Three men go to M.G. course at Camiers. One gunner to hospital injured.	
"	25		Very fine. Some overhead fire. Wind S.E. 2000 rounds.	
"	26		Very fine & hot. Wind S & S.W. Thiepval & Combles fallen. Aeroplane activity. Night-firing from C.19.a.2.3 on to C.7.a.2½.1 3000 rounds.	
"	27		Overhead fire from C.19.a.2.5 on to C.7.a.2½.3 & C.7.a.8½.3. 700 rounds. Back fire with K.N.15 broke the extractor grooves. Hostile bombing party assailed sap East of C.13.c.2½.½ approximately at C.7.d. Fine but light showers in afternoon. Wind S.W. Enemy aeroplanes overhead.	

B.H.O'N

Army Form C. 2118.

WAR DIARY
or
INTELLIGENCE SUMMARY
(Erase heading not required.)

Place	Date	Hour	Summary of Events and Information	Remarks and references to Appendices
YPRES SALIENT	28		Wind East & S.E. Very fine & warm. Raid by 13 R.W.F. between 11.30 & 12 midnight. Operations: Overhead fire from C.13.C.2.8, placing barrage over C.14 central. 1750 rounds of which were fired between 11.30 & midnight. 750 rounds fired from E.27 (C.13.b.7.3) as barrage across No Man's Land on to C.14.a.3.6. between 11.30 & midnight. 250 rounds fired from C.14.c.7.6 burst across No Man's Land on right of raiding party on to C.14.a.8½.2 traversing 25° East. Muzzle cup jammed badly causing 15' stoppage of fire.	
"	29		Wind E. & N.E. strong. No.4002 Saxby W. sent to BASE under escort. Hostile Trench mortars active on our left & round C.7.c.2½.½	
"	30		Wind N.E. Hostile Trench mortars round C.14.c.3.4 & C.7.c.2.3. Time put back one hour at midnight. No.23665 Pte Baxter J.	

R.H.B. Ashurn

Vol 6

WAR DIARY.

113 MACHINE GUN COY.

OCTOBER 1916.

WAR DIARY or INTELLIGENCE SUMMARY

Army Form C. 2118.

113 M.G.C.

October

Place	Date	Hour	Summary of Events and Information	Remarks and references to Appendices
YPRES SALIENT	1		At 12.59 A.M. Winter Shoot commenced. Hostile O.B. set on fire by British battle plane 8.50 A.M. One man on cold shooting course. Wind EASTERLY. Enemy brought down BELGIUM O.B.	
"	2		1000 rounds fired from C.19.a.14.3 overhead searching on to B.13.6.9.9 – C.1.C.7.2½. 1000 rounds overhead from C.13.a.3.6 on to cross roads C.2.C.8.8 traversing to IRON CROSS. 1000 rounds fired from C.13.C.2.3 indirect overhead on to C.15.C.4.7. All night firing above working party of this company dispersed without casualty by hostile trench mortars. Enemy near C.14.a used a small search light. GAS ALERT off. Wind S.W. cold & rain all day. Alert on again at 9.30 P.M. Wind S.E. veering to W. at night. Wind reported SAFE.	
"	3		Rain most of day. Stunt overhead night firing as on the 2nd. Enemy trench mortared posts around C.14.C.3.4 & C.14.C.9.1. Twenty yards from C.7.C.O.2. enemy sent two rumjars that broke trench in. Most trenchmortaring noticed front line positions. Enemy sent a bombing post N.N.V.E.29 but was bombed out soon. Our trench mortars shelled enemy lines this afternoon heavily. Switchboard sent at P3a (C.7.C.O.2) during this bombardment.	
"	4		Same overhead night firing as on 3rd inst. Hostile T.M. broke in dugout at P3a (C.7.C.O.2), occupants got out. Our man 26971 Pte GAVIN slight shrapnel wound on arm. Wind West & reported safe. At 7.30 slight southerly disturbance with rain. Wind Dangerous. Rest of day wind West & safe, with rain.	
"	5		Wind N.W. & W. Strong. Gun at C.19.a.14.3 fired 1000 rounds same target as on 2nd Gun at C.13.a.3.4 fired 1000 rounds on to C.7.C.2.7. Hostile T.M. fire on to C.19.6.3.8 Defence on post at C.7.C.O.2 removed to P13 (C.13.a.3.4) One man from hospital sick	
"	6		All quiet; no overhead night firing. One to hospital sick	

73. R. Dallas Lt.
for Major 73. H. Badham
O.C. 113 N.G.Coy.
Sch C. S. M.
M. G. Coy.

Army Form C. 2118.

113 M.G.C. 2

WAR DIARY
or
INTELLIGENCE SUMMARY
(Erase heading not required.)

October

Place	Date	Hour	Summary of Events and Information	Remarks and references to Appendices
YPRES SALIENT	7		Same overhead fire as on 2.10.16. 3000 rounds. Stiff West wind	
"	8		Wind W. by N. Stiff. Our man to hospital, our man from hospital. German seen 100ft from our wire at 5.30 A.M. at C.13.a.7.8; on being challenged, came in as prisoner. Information gathered from him to effect that our searching fires about 2000x caused a certain amount of difficulties on roads & occasional casualties. Hostile shelling on Ypres-Yser bank.	
"	9		Gun at C.19.a.2.2½ fired 500 rounds on to C.7.a.2.1 " " C.13.C.3.2. " 800 " " C.15.a.4.7 Wind fresh & WEST. Hostile M.G. fire reported bringing an aeroplane down.	
"	10		Fresh wind W. to N.W. Our artillery had a shoot 2.30 to 5.30. 3. 31093 2/Opl 2/Cpl. POVAH, & 26703 Pte PAYNE sent to TBASE, excess of establishment. 2nd Lt. T.E. FITZGERALD & Pte No.2/5/8 R.M. EVANS to England on leave.	
"	11		Indirect searching fire from C.19.a.9.8½ to A.7.a.2.0 & A.7.a.9.5. 580 rounds fired. Enemy M.G. fire fairly active over BR'DGE 6Z.	
"	12		Operations: Gun at C.13.6.3.2½ fired 1000 rounds between 9.p. & 9.30 P.M. 1000 rounds at normal rate through the night towards KRUPPS FARM searching 14B. in enfilade. Gun at C.14.C.6.8 fired 500 rounds as barrage across No Mans Land between the hours of 9.1½ & 9.30 P.M. in direction C.14.a.8.0. Gun at C.13.6.8.4 fired 1250 rounds as barrage across No Mans Land on to C.14.a.1.7. Enemy M.G. fire very clear over gun at C.13.6.3.2½. These operations were carried out in conjunction with a successful raid by the 13TH.W.F. who mounted prisoners one Gunner, a Prussian M.Gunner & took the Guns, similar machine to our Maxim, with a accidental scuth by which the strength of the Fusn. Spring could be noted & fired with precision	

B.R. Dibbs Lt.
O.C. 113 M.G. Coy.
N.G. Corps.

Army Form C. 2118.

113 M.G.C.
October

WAR DIARY or INTELLIGENCE SUMMARY
(Erase heading not required.)

Place	Date	Hour	Summary of Events and Information	Remarks and references to Appendices
YPRES SALIENT	13		Operations: Gun at C.19.a.2.3½ fired between 8 & 8.15 P.M. 750 rounds fire on to C.14.c.4.5½.	
			" " " " 8.15 & 8.35 " 3750 "	
			" " " " 8.35 & 9.15 " 1750 " as indirect enfilade.	
			Gun at C.19.a.4.9 fired as barrage towards C.7.d. between 8.14 & 8.45 P.M. 1250 rounds	
			Gun at C.13.a.6.9 fired as barrage across No Man's Land towards C.8.c. between 8.14 & 8.55 P.M. 1450 rounds.	
			Intelligence: 11 "duds" out of 23 hostile medium shells were fired in vicinity of BRIDGE 6D. Some of our trenches suffered from hostile shellings also BRIDGE 6D.	
			Enemy used a searchlight from the CANAL BANK on our left searching towards C.13.a.6.9. Red, Green & yellow rockets were sent up by the enemy at 8.10 P.M. Enemy used more artillery than T.M's during the Raid. The Vickers guns at C.14.c.4.9 & C.13.a.6.9 were subjected to a somewhat severe rifle grenade & shell fire. Three guns were in action during a successful raid by the XV R.W.F. (Royden Welsh) who took 4 prisoners Prussian Guard. No. 26702 WELLS W.G. Evacuated on munitions. Gun sick to hospital.	
"	14		Gun at C.19.a.8.1½ fired 2000 rounds in enfilade over C.14.a.4.5½ of the enemy front line. Used as "rapid" by the enemy T.M. bombardment. Enemy T.M's during this bombardment took place from 12 noon to 1.30 P.M. Enemy sent up white rockets during this bombardment. At C.7.C.24.5½ hostile T.M. blew one of the gun team No. 31963 Pte PRICE H. out of the trench into No Man's Land at 1.40 P.M. Two men went over & fetched him in taking about five minutes & not having a shot fired at them. Pte Price died at 4 P.M. in hospital. Sergeant HOLBERT No. M/8? slight hip wound who fetched Price in returned to duty. Gun sick to hospital. Three returned from M.G. course. No. 24698 Cpl Simms, No. 236881 Pte MILTON & No. 2368? Pte Durlacher. G	B.T.R. Dalbos Lt. O.C. 113 M.G.Coy. B.T.R. Dalbos Lt. O.C. 113 M.G.Coy. M.G. Corps.

Army Form C. 2118.

113 M.G.C.

October

4.

WAR DIARY
or
INTELLIGENCE SUMMARY
(Erase heading not required.)

Place	Date	Hour	Summary of Events and Information	Remarks and references to Appendices
YPRES SALIENT	15		Wind still WEST, slightly overcast. Enemy fired one shell over BRIELEN, one over ELVERDINGHE, & one on CANAL BANK at about noon. Relief by day taking place. All firing quiet. The Coy. was relieved by the 115 M.G. Coy. by day. The last team was relieved at 7.10 P.M. when hostile guns of all calibre shelled roads, the villages, Canal Bank & faith trenches at varying intervals just at the hour when transport was on many roads. A few casualties. Everything points to the day relief having been observed this survey. One to hospital sick; two from hospital.	
A.22.d.5.3	16.		In CAMP "S" a.22.d.8.3. One mule evacuated veterinary reasons. First animal evacuated since the company came out.	
"	17.		Raining. Wind N.W. Lt. F.H. CHAMPION went to the 90 M.G. Coy. as 2nd i/c.	
"	18.		Wind N.N.W. 2/Lt. TAYLOR went to hospital sick. Rain all day. One man sick to hospital. 2/Lt. C.J. MORTON & Sergt. GARDNER sent to GAS School.	
"	19		Heavy rain all day & night. 2/Lt. F.C. TAYLOR sent to No.10 C.C.S. Sergt. HOLBERT to hospital Cold night. Wind N.E. & DANGEROUS.	
"	20		Bright, clear, & cold. Wind EAST. Aeroplane activity. Frost in early morning.	
"	21		Fine, cold EAST wind. Frost at night. Major B.H. BADHAM sent to Corps school. Hostile aeroplanes with Allies markings brought down at O.B. Two men to hospital sick. Cold, S.E. wind & bright. One to hospital. 2/Lt. Morton & Sergt. Gardner return from Gas School.	
"	22.		Wind S. WEST. Raining. Lt. T.E. FITZGERALD returned from leave. 2/Lt. A.H. BOTLER to hospital & D.R.S.	
"	23.		Major B.H. BADHAM sent to Lt. TOOGOOD Lewis Gun School. Wind S. West & rainy.	
"	24.		Lt. HIBBERT C.B. appointed C.O. of this company from 55. M.G.Coy. All Guns etc. sent up to this line for tomorrows nights relief. Wind SAFE. One sick to hospital. Two from hospital	B.T. Dr. 105 Lt. O.C. 113 M.G. Coy. 113 M.G. Corps.

Army Form C. 2118.

113 M.G.C.
October

WAR DIARY or INTELLIGENCE SUMMARY
(Erase heading not required.)

Place	Date	Hour	Summary of Events and Information	Remarks and references to Appendices
Rest Camp A.22.d.4.5	25		Lt. T. E. FITZGERALD sent to VIII Corps School. Camp cleaned up & Company left for the trenches at 4 P.M. arriving at 200x distances by sections at 6.30 P.M. All guns in position by 10 P.M. A quiet night. Rain all day with S.W. wind.	
Ypres Salient	26		Building Kitchens, cookhouses etc. Rainy P.M. most of the day. A strong W. wind was blowing. Gun at C.13.a.3½.½ fired 2000 rounds on to Farm 14 (C20.50). During bombardment of the enemy lines about C.7.C.8.7. Gun at C.7.C.2.3 was removed during a T.M. bombardment. Pte. BAXTER J. returned from leave to U.K. One man to hospital sick; two from hospital. No. 28665 Pte BAXTER J. 1000 rounds between	
"	27		Gun at C.19.a.2.2 fired 2500 rounds at noon on 26 C.7.a.4.2. & 1000 rounds between 4 & 5.30 A.M. Wind strong S.W. fine. Enemy artillery T.M. more active at noon. Lt. B.R. DEEDES appointed C.O. of 2nd M.G. Coy.	
"	28		Strong S.S.W. wind, overcast & showery. Operations during Raid by the 1673rd R.W.F. at 11-20 P.M. Owing to the extreme quiet request in Enemy line some M.G. fire was brought to bear from two of our guns at request of C.O. 16 73rd R.W.F.	
"	29		*Direct fire.* Gun at B.12.c.8.5 fired from 11-20 to midnight 1750 rounds barrage across No Mans Land on to recentrant at C.7.c. 1.92 " C.7.c.12.6 " " " 2500 " " nose at C.7.c.22.9 " C.7.c.6½.3 " " " 2500 " " Fortin 17 at C.7.d.6.7 *Overhead Indirect* Gun at C.19.a.2.2½ fired 1000 rounds on to trenches C.14.6. between 9. & 11 P.M. from 11-20 to 12-5 A.M. 2000 rounds on to GERMAN Sap at C.7.d.5.7 " 12.5 " 3. A.M. 1000 " C.13.c.3.2 fired 750 rounds on to trenches C.8.d. central from 9. to 10-45 P.M. from 11-25 to 11-44 P.M. 850 rounds on to x roads at C.t.C.3.2 traversing 15° EAST. " 11-55 to 3. A.M. 900 "	B.T.C. D. lloyd lt. Lt. G. Coys. O.C. 113 M.G.C.

2449 Wt. W14957/M90 750,000 1/16 J.B.C. & A. Forms/C.2118/12.

Army Form C. 2118.

113 N.G. Coy.
October

WAR DIARY
or
INTELLIGENCE SUMMARY
(Erase heading not required.)

Place	Date	Hour	Summary of Events and Information	Remarks and references to Appendices
Ypres Salient	29 (continued)		Gun at C.19.a.2.2. fired from 11·20 to 11·44 P.M. 750 rounds ⎱ searchlights vertically up CABLE LANE ⎰ from C.7.a.8.4 to C.7.a.8·10 " 11·55 " 3. A.M. 1000 " ⎱ from C.7.a.8·4 to C.7.a.8·10 ⎰ 500° from the GERMAN trenches. The gun at B.12.d.8.3 was placed in an old disused French trench 500° from the GERMAN trenches to be entered & was apparently never discovered, once again emphasising the superiority of the searching screen over the "stove pipe." The gun at C.7.c.6½.3 was placed amongst our wire in an old shell hole. A piece of corrugated iron was placed at a steep angle on the enfilade finish to stop mud & pieces of stone from shell bursts. This gun was in a very secure position with its exposed right flank somewhat protected by the overhead sun at C.7.a.2.t firing on to Sap at C.7.d.3.7. A box of No. 19 grenades was kept near at hand. A large white tape was laid from the communication trench to this position to guide ammunition carriers to the team on its way back. A lamp slung on the knees by the canal could not be seen from this position. In all guns one muzzle cup broken 2 lock spring broken were the only stoppages caused besides one t old belt - lose pockets. 2/Lt HISTRAY all 4/5 Scottish Rifles arrived. S.W. wind from 60 to 70 m.p.h. Showery.	
"	30		Wind S.W. strong, showery. Hostile shelling on front line. M.G. post at C.7.c.2.3 somewhat battered about. A quiet night. Lt. C.D. HIBBERT arrived to take command.	
"	31		Lt. T.E. FITZGERALD appointed 2nd I/C of 116 M.G.C.	

B.R. Drake Lt.
O.C. 113 M.G.C.

WAR DIARY

FOR

NOVEMBER 1916

Vol 7

113 MACHINE GUN COMPANY.

WAR DIARY or INTELLIGENCE SUMMARY

Army Form C. 2118.

of 113th Machine Gun Company,
B.E.F.

Sheet 1.

Place	Date	Hour	Summary of Events and Information	Remarks and references to Appendices
YPRES SALIENT (LEFT SECTOR) 4 LEFT Inf: Bde: Rly: ST JULIEN 28 N.W.	1.XI.16		Wind. S.W. backing to S. Weather. Showery. SICK REPORT. 26690 Pte Hanley. S. 34881 Pte Welsh. R. 27444 Pte Brigham. W. 2/231 Pte Cunnell. J. all to Hosp:ᴸ Attached from 54472 Pte Ashworth.W. 21966 Pte Woods. J. 21940 " Attwood. W. 15/R.W.F. 54477 " Parrish. F. Ret: 2/Lt Capt: Butler from Hospᴸ to 10. C.C.S. 7/Lt J.C. Taylor to U.K. (Sick). 7/Lt D. Vale. Reinforcement from Base. ST JULIEN MAP. 28N.W. OPERATIONS. Gun at C19.c.3.2 fired 2000 Rounds on Cable Lane. C7.b.1.6 NORTHWARDS. INTELLIGENCE. Post at F3 demolished by enemy shells. Gun was temporarily withdrawn to P.a. (49.c.13.a.3.6?) when enemy C7.c.2.3. position was shewn. During hostile bombardment in Left Sector of Bde. area, Green and Red Rockets were observed rising from WEST of CANAL de L'YSER.	
"	2.XI.16		Wind. S.W. Weather. Showery. Sunshine. SICK REPORT. 26706 Pte Bottom. L. from Hospᴸ 42470 " Reid. J. to Hospᴸ B.E.F. Lt B.R. Dollors left this unit to take up Command of 21/M.G.Coy. Attached from 34663 Pte Burrows. B. 23136 Pte Hughes. R. 13/R.W.F. 17472 " Morgan. B. 44796 " Marsh. F.W. Operations. Gun at C19.3 fired on CABLE LANE (C7.a.7.4. to C7.a.8?.10) 1500 Rnds. INTELLIGENCE Enemy trench mortars on left rather intense. ARTILLERY active. - at B12.b.7o. (French line) small patrol of enemy crossed CANAL on a raft: threw a few bombs on French sentry posts: and withdrew in safety returning on raft. 9 British aeroplanes flew over German lines in the afternoon. Enemy opened shell and M.G. fire on them in vain.	
"	3.XI.16		Wind. Backed to S. Weather. Fine generally. SICR: 21940 Pte Atwood. R. 15/R.W.F. to Hospᴸ At 2.0.p.m. An observation balloon was seen drifting on the wind in a N.E. direction. Artillery on both sides fired on it with no result (apparently). It passed out of sight over enemy's line. Incidentally "Zone" an aeroplane reported balloon coming down in NORWAY in this day.	

(signed) Challoner
Lt. 113th M.G.C.
O/c 113th M.G.C.

Army Form C. 2118.

WAR DIARY
or
INTELLIGENCE SUMMARY
(Erase heading not required.)

113th.I.G.Coy.
B.E.F.

Sheet 1

Instructions regarding War Diaries and Intelligence Summaries are contained in F.S. Regs., Part II. and the Staff Manual respectively. Title Pages will be prepared in manuscript.

Place	Date	Hour	Summary of Events and Information	Remarks and references to Appendices
YPRES SALIENT. Ref: SJ 14-16N, 26 N.W.	4.XI.16		WIND. S. 6.30.p.m. WIND DANGEROUS. 9.0.p.m. WIND SAFE. Weather. Clear. Sunshine. SICK. 26979 Ypl.Colley.A. 26975 Pt. Norton.A. Both to Hosp.S. 42141 Ypl Mickleburgh.A. Bullet wound in thigh at D1 C14c 9.1½ presumably from a sniper. OPERATIONS. Inter-section relief took place. Completed by 6.0.p.m. Gun at C.14.3 fired on CACTUS AVENUE (C.7.6.1.6 NORTHWARDS to REY) 4000 Rnds. Gun at C19c 3.2 fired 2000 Rnds on BOURNIER F.d. C9d 2.7 and trench running to C9d 6 2.0. (Firing during night but guns) D3 C19c 2045 trench mortars). No damage done. Occasional M.G. fire (enemy) from CANAL de L'YSER.	
	5.XI.16		WIND. S.W. WEATHER. Showery. SICK. Nil. OPERATIONS. Gun at C19.3 fired 2000 Rnds on CACTUS AVENUE + NORTHWARDS between 6.30pm — 10.30pm 5/6.XI.16 and 1.0am — 3.0am 6.XI.16. Gun at C13c.3.2 fired 2500 Rnds on Tramway junction C14.B.6.9 to pt C9c 10.15 between 8.0.Pm — 12.0 midnight 5/6.XI.16 and 1.0am — 2.0am 6.XI.16. 3645 36/21 Driver White E. from Base (Reinforcement) INTELLIGENCE. CAPTAIN C.R. HIBBERT on leave to U.K. 5.XI.16 — 15.XI.16.	
	6.XI.16		WIND. S.W. WEATHER. Cold. Showery. SICK. 19297 Pt. Bich F. 16/R.W.F. from 26989 "Russell.C." } Hope? Attached: 21881 Pt. Alley G. to this unit from 15/R.W.F. 9/Lt. C.F. Norton to M.G. Course, CAMIERS. 54824 Pt. Armstrong G. Machine Gunner Reinforcement OPERATIONS. Gun at C13c 3.2 fired 2000 Rnds on CROSS ROADS, PILCKEM C1 c 85.80 from Base. to GAS BARRIER H. C2 60.5 INTELLIGENCE. at 1.0 p.m. and at 3.0.p.m. our artillery put over several salvoes presumably on ENEMY WORKING PARTIES.	
	7.XI.16		WIND. SW to N.W. WEATHER. Fine. Cold. Sunshine. SICK. 26701 Pt. Sheppard. G. Hosp.S. (D/A.H). 5035 Pt Sutciren W. Sniper's bullet through left shoulder. INTELL: Gun Emplacements withdrawn on 1.XI.16 to C13a 3.6½ moved in BUTT 22, C13a 55.40. G.O.C's ORDER. C13a 36½.	

Vandeleur (signature)
O/C 113 Coy M.G.C

Vandeleur (signature)
NOC 113 M.G.C.

2449 Wt. W14957/M90 750,000 1/16 J.B.C. & A. Forms/C.2118/12.

Army Form C. 2118

WAR DIARY
or
INTELLIGENCE SUMMARY
(Erase heading not required.)

113 m/gun
BEF.

Sheet III

Place	Date	Hour	Summary of Events and Information	Remarks and references to Appendices
YPRES SALIENT. Ref: ST JULIEN. 28 N.W.	8.XI.16		WIND. S.W. WEATHER. Rain on 7.XI.16. SICK. 22470 Pte. Reid. J. from Hosp^l. OPERATIONS- Reinforcement from Base. 7/Lt. O. Benson. 6. G.C.1.D.1.S between 8.30pm and 3.0am following morning. Gun at C.19.3 fired 2000 Rnds on R4 B.12.8.8 Lt. Pt. C.1.D.1.S between 8.30pm and 3.0am following morning. Ennied store found at F.3. C.7.C.2.3 valued & taken to Butt 22 C.13a SS.40. INTELLI: noening to N.W. WEATHER. First morning and evening. Iris. SICK. 27444 Pte Bingham W. } from Hosp^l. 11855 Cpl Fleming R. }	
	9.XI.16		WIND. S.W. WEATHER. Completed by 6.15 p.m. Bombing post No.5. 13/2 2.69 was taken over from Infantry. Gun formerly at Pl. C.13a 3.4. Though in close proximity to enemy and in dangerous INTELLI: position, this is a position of great advantage: able to enfilade Boche front line and fire along M.L. C.7.c.area. 3. Two enemy aeroplanes over own lines (left sector) at 3.30 p.m. Shelled by us without success.	
	10.XI.16		WIND. Almost nil. S.W. tany. WEATHER. Frosts in Early a.m. Clean. Sunshine. SICK. { 7/Lt C.I.Norton (on Commission M.G. Corps) to Hosp^l. 28080 Pte Howe. J. to Hosp^l (Inflt) 26949 " Heaton.W. " " 42470 " Reid . T . " (P.U.0) LEAVE. 23688 Pte Hilton.S. from U.K. (granted 5 days Satisfaction). 2201 Pte Scott G.C. to U.K. (11.xi.16 – 21.xi.16) OPERATIONS. In conjunction with Trench Mortar Stafge on left. C.19.3 fired 2000 Rnds on CANAL AVENUE (Pt. C.7a.3.0 to C.7a.7.2.9) initial Search. C.19.2 fired 2000 Rnds on CABLE LANE (C.7a 7.3½ 76 C.1C.8.0). Gun at C.13.c.3.2 fired 2300 Rnds on CACTUS AVENUE C.7.6.1.6 to C.7.d.7.5.4. In each case Normal fire was opened at 10.0 p.m. from 11.0 – 11.45 p.m. Gun fired RAPID and then Resumed Normal until 11.40 p.m when they ceased fire. 16/R.W.F. did not warn unit of return of their Patrol (time of exit 11.45 p.m) so fire was not resumed. At 10.0 p.m. Gun at No.5 Bombing Post was withdrawn to place of safety nr BOESINGHE. (G.O.C's order). Post was Reoccupied by Gun at 12.0 midnight. INTELL: 1. Enemy made no determined or organised interference to the Strage. Their artillery were active during 3.0pm. -4.0am. 2. Enemy aircraft were very much during morning at great altitude.	
	11.XI.16		WIND. Mild. S.W. WEATHER. Fine generally. SICK. 26690 Pte Hanley S. from Hosp^l. 13728 " depot F. to 15 C.C.S. 26691 " Kneeton A.R. to Hosp^l (Bails). Pat No.5. and trench in vicinity blown in by enemy Trench Mortar. Gun was buried but not damaged. No casualties. Working party was sent up from H.Q. to rebuild emplacement and to clear trench. This was done by 3.0 am of 12.xi.16.	Shellock Lt M. O. C. 113. M/gun Corps M OC 113 m/gC

2449 Wt. W14957/M90 750,000 1/16 J.B.C. & A. Forms/C.2118/12.

WAR DIARY or INTELLIGENCE SUMMARY

Army Form C. 2118.

113 Inf Bde
B.E.F.

Sheet IV.

Place	Date	Hour	Summary of Events and Information	Remarks and references to Appendices
YPRES SALIENT. Ref: ST JULIEN 28 N.W.	12.XI.16		WIND. S.W. to W. WEATHER Fine. SICK. NIL. OPERATIONS. Gun at C.13.A.c.3.2. fired 2000 Rnds on CANDLE AVENUE (at C.8.b.40.85. to M.C.3.c.15.80.) Trench was enfiladed at occasional intervals between 6.0 p.m. – 7.0 p.m. and 10.15 p.m. – 3.0 a.m. following morning.	
	13.XI.16		WIND. Practically nil. WEATHER. Fine. Visibility bad. SICK. 26961 Pte Hinton W. to D.R.S. 42470. " Reid. J " " " Reinforcement from Base. { 13346 Pte Moore. S. 27604 " Norton. J. 27356 Pte Mason H. } Nil incident at CHEAPSIDE O.P from 12.0 noon to 3.0 p.m. WEATHER. Fine. Frost in evening.	
	14.XI.16.		WIND. N.E. to E. WIND DANGEROUS. 6.30 a.m. SICK. 21940 Pte Haines R.W. from Hosp. 15/R.W.F. 21966 " Ashwood W. To Hosp. (P.U.O.) 15/R.W.F.	
YPRES	15.XI.16		INTELL: At 1.40 p.m. Enemy aeroplane flew over our lines and destroyed an observation balloon, afterwards returning in safety. Observer descents in his parachute. Enemy aeroplane was over our line during the night; and morning of the 15.XI.16. Between 2.0 p.m. and 2.45 p.m. Heavy artillery registered on BOSCHE Front line about 250 yards S of CAESAR'S NOSE.	
			WIND. N.E. to E. WEATHER. Frosty morning. v. clear sunshine. SICK. { 34881 Pte Welch R. from Hosp. 26701 Pte Sheppard N.G. to 46 C.C.S.} 44706. " Mead. F.W. to Hosp. 13/R.W.F.	
Ref: BELGIUM 28 N.W. Sq. 3D	16.XI.16.		During the afternoon and evening 113 M.G. Coy returned to "S" Camp A.22.d.9.3. "S" CAMP. A.22.d.9.3.	
"S" CAMP. A.22.d.9.3.			WIND. E. WEATHER. CRISP. FROSTY. Very cold. A little sunshine. SICK. 26979 4/Cpl Colley H. (from Hosp?) LEAVE 14275 C.S.M. Rogers E. home to U.K. (16.XI.16 – 26.XI.16) 11261 Sgt Holbert. S. to be acting C.S.M. until further notice. COURSE 4.2288 Sgt Kerr W. to go Course "H" Camp. Arms and some parts of L.V. Section to ORDNANCE for overhauling.	

Churchill Capt
O/C 113 Inf Bde for O.C. 113 L.M.G.C.

WAR DIARY or INTELLIGENCE SUMMARY

Army Form C. 2118.

113 M.G. Coy.
B.E.F.

Sheet V.

Place	Date	Hour	Summary of Events and Information	Remarks and references to Appendices
'S' CAMP.	17.XI.16.		WIND. E. WEATHER. COLD. FROST. SICK. 26690 Pte Hanley. E. to Hosp. } (Dent)	
	18.XI.16.		WIND. E to S.E. 26691 Pte Laster a.R. } from Hosp. 2966 " Ashwood W. LEAVE. CAPTAIN. C.B. HIBAE Kt. from U.K. (2 days extension). Reorganisation and sorting of material. Men taken at Div. Bath. As Central.	
	19.XI.16.		WIND. S. WEATHER. Fine snow day. CHURCH PARADES: WORKING PARTIES at YPRES PRISON. No parades except Rifle Inspection. 115 M.G. Guy's Horse Lines	
	20.XI.16.		WIND. S. WEATHER. Drizzle milder. WORKING PARTIES. BRICK GATHERING at YPRES PRISON: CABLE BURYING in LINE. 115 M.G. HORSE STANDINGS: Billet building in camp.	
	21.XI.16.		WIND. S. WEATHER. Fine. Mist in late afternoon. LEAVE. 2/Lr A.M. Rivas to U.K. 21.XI.16 to 1.XII.16. SICK. 14247 Pte Reid. T. } Storm Hospl. 21231 " Cunnah. J.T. }	
	22.XI.16.		WIND. S. WEATHER. Con d SICK. Nil. No English mail.	
			COURSE. 2/Lr W.tonight to CORPS SCHOOL (22.XI.16) (-20.XII.16) 42418 Pte Smith N.R. (Batman)	
	23.XI.16		WIND. S/6 S.W. Weather Dull. SICK. 26698 Cpl Simms W. to Hosp. tont P.U.O. Pres. 295.18 Evans R.M. and 29558. Batty. R.P. } of 16th RW3/16 England to Officers Castleland	
	24.XII.16		Wins S/5 S.W. Weather Dull. Sick Report Nil. Guns sent up with advance party to Canal Bank. Appointment LT. C.Bullock appointed 2nd in Command 101 M.G.C.	
	25.XI.16		WIND. S.W. Weather C/8/5 wet. Sick report Nil. Company Left S. Camp at 3.30 p.m marching in sections at 10 mts interval. Relieved 115 M.G.C. in line. Relief completed 9.40 p.m.	

C. Bullock Lt
for O.C. 113 M.G. Coy

J.B.M. Westgarth Capt
O.C. 113 Coy M.G.C.

WAR DIARY / INTELLIGENCE SUMMARY

Army Form C. 2118

Sheet VI.   113 M.G.C.

Place	Date	Hour	Summary of Events and Information	Remarks and references to Appendices
Camp Bus/S	26.11.16		Wind S.W. Weather cold. Sick report Nil. Leave Nos 23136 Hughes R. 23743 Hardy B.S. and 20907 Arkingstall R. on leave (10 days) to U.K. Operations Nil. Intelligence Nil.	
"	27.11.16		Wind S.W. Weather cold. Dangerous Gas alarm but no gas followed. Weather foggy all day. Sick report 11864 Pte Whyte to Hospital. Course of Musk. Vale M.G. Course at Carriers. No 43105 Pte Shelton went with M.Vale. Operations Nil. Intelligence (a) From 1.15 p.m. to 2 p.m. enemy shelled C.13 d. Fi. 6. without effect. About 15% of his shells fell & exploded. Renewed shelling from 9.30 to 10 p.m. in same position. No damage reported. (b) D bridge also reported as enemy target from 1.15 to 2 p.m.	
"	28.11.16		Wind S.W. Weather cold & foggy. Sick report 19-9 Pte Fold. to Hospital. 38761 Sg. Teakle & 70 Hospital. Strength 2/Lieut. V & I. Dg Donald reported for duty. Operations Nil. Intelligence Nil. Vigorous enemy shelling from 7.25 to 9.0 p.m.	
"	29.11.16		Wind S.W. Weather cold & foggy. D.l. C.M. C.G.'s blown in and some buried. Emplacement at C.M. C.G.'s blown in and some buried but soon restored. all material kept good parts kept. Sick report Nil. Strength Lieut. C.R. Robinson reported on duty. Operations Nil Intelligence Nil.	
"	30.11.16		Intelligence Nil.	

Shelford [?]
2/Lieut. O.C.
O.C. 113 M.G.C.

115th MACHINE GUN COY. Vol 8

WAR DIARY

FOR

DECEMBER 1916

WAR DIARY or INTELLIGENCE SUMMARY

Army Form C. 2118.

(Erase heading not required.)

Place	Date	Hour	Summary of Events and Information	Remarks and references to Appendices
	1/12/16 2/12/16		Company in trenches CANAL BANK Sector YPRES. Enemy Quiet. Enemy Quiet. Enemy M.Guns active during night. Enfiled 750.25 on C.2.B.85.10	
	3/12/16		Enemy snipers on left of sector at midnight. Great on Indirect O.L. Ent. gunfire by shellfire - Casualty - one Gun at C.13.6.10.40 also on L ration party dumps at Enemy artillery active in Rt sector.	one man killed
	4/12/16		Enemy snipers CANAL BANK HORNBY CITY with Lgd Vickery Shell - provide application five Quiet 2000 rds on enemy Turrettes from ALBERT ROAD 13 C.7.b.6.0.4 Lt/Rhodes sick C.C.S.	
	5/12/16		Enemy artillery Rifle active in our front lines on HINDENBERG FRONT - quiet.	
	6/12/16		Enemy Quiet. After heavy shells fell near LANCASHIRE FARM Reinforcements - 5.	
	7/12/16		Enemy artillery active - on artillery retaliated fire Bull reported woods intermittently Lcm 7in3 o.t Lwis Gun	
	8/12/16		Enemy Quiet. The hunt mentioned enemy front	
	9/12/16		Enemy artillery retaliation arranged for our Jt Fr gun – Lt/Comm Jones found 5015 4.5 on enemy Supports	
	10/12/16		Right dismounted artillery active in long Night	Pte 36623 Williamson promoted to unpaid L/Cpl
	11/12/16		Enemy artillery Quiet - on aeroplanes active M.Comm forwarded at same H.K.	
	12/12/16		Relieved by 117 Reg co. - After relief billets night 11/12/16 - in POPERINGHE.	
	13/12/16 14/12/16 15/		Entrained for BOULEZELE their Camp 8 trenches. Daily training in Company. Physical Drill, Advances, Rifle exercises.	
	23/12/16 24/12/16		Open warfare General Training.	
	24/12/16 25/12/16 26/12/16 27/12/16 30/12/16 31/12/16		Inspected by C.O.C. Gen Sir D. Haig. Transferred to Hindu to the O.H. Cpt. Houghton procured leave for Comm. Ft Sealey, O.C Comd Hutton Capt Slatter Jd Robinson procured on Ft Course at Cape School. Training in open warfare Arrival of Ft Vinnicombe. Coy proceeded by road from BOULEZELE to "G" Camp YPRES.	

2449 Wt. W14957/M90 750,000 1/16 J.B.C. & A. Forms/C.2118/12.

WAR DIARY

FOR

JANUARY 1917

113 MACHINE GUN COMPANY

Vol 9

WAR DIARY
or
INTELLIGENCE SUMMARY

Army Form C. 2118.

113th Machine Gun Coy —

Place	Date	Hour	Summary of Events and Information	Remarks and references to Appendices
YPRES SECTOR	1/1/17		Coy in reserve "Vlatercots" "J" Camp.	
	2/1/17		General M.G. Training	
	3/1/17		General M.G. Training with tactical schemes range practice. Working party Elverdinghe	
	4/1/17		do	
	5/1/17		do	
	6/1/17		do — J.O.K. on leave U.K.	
	7/1/17		Church parade + Inspection. Knight Capt. 8th Corps VII Corps School. Competition Football Match.	
	8/1/17		General M.G. Training. Lecture on Gas — J.O.K. leave to U.K.	
	9/1/17		" range work + night work — working party 10 YPRES. Enemy aeroplanes active	
	10/1/17		Whole Coy practices hanging live bombs under Bn Bombing Officer. Working party 6 YPRES.	
	11/1/17		Coy training + physical. Range work. Needlewing games Pumbers	
	12/1/17		+ Tactical scheme	
	13/1/17		General training. Working party + Church parade.	
	14/1/17		Inspections + Church parade. Preparation for Winter	
	15/1/17		Coy moved into CANAL BANK trenches relieved 117 M.G. Co. Lt Bullock + 2 O.R. leave U.K.	
	16/1/17		Enemy artillery machine guns quiet. Snowstorm. 13 below zero. 3 in reserve.	
	17/1/17		Enemy quiet — we fired 2000 rds indirect fire on enemy C. trenches — full of snow	
	18/1/17		Enemy M.G. active during night. We fired 1500 rds on enemy lines	
	19/1/17		Intermittent enemy shelling. Inspected armoured train active belong our line during evening. Heavy artillery fire during evening on our lines.	
	20/1/17		Frost. Snow still on the ground. Our artillery active during morning	
	21/1/17		3 cmdy. Intermittent enemy shelling. Enemy active with machine guns fire during afternoon + evening.	
	22/1/17		Frosty. Enemy M. guns active during night. Intermittent enemy shelling.	
	23/1/17		Frosty. Enemy aircraft active over our lines during afternoon. Lt Robinson + 2 O.R. leave U.K.	
	24/1/17		Relieved by 196th M.G. Coy. 113th returning to B.13.A.50.60.	
	24/1/17		Frosty. Clearing up — overhauling of Lanteuns, guns + C + improvements to camp (B.13A 50.60.)	
	25/1/17		Frosty. General M.G. Training with Tactical schemes. Accoutrering + replacing Elver Ample + L	
			Luce Alternet.	

Army Form C. 2118.

WAR DIARY
or
INTELLIGENCE SUMMARY
(Erase heading not required.)

Place	Date	Hour	Summary of Events and Information	Remarks and references to Appendices
YPRES SECTOR	26.1.17		General Machine Gun Training & Tactical Scheme. Frosty weather. Test alarm – manning of line & Thievenghe Defences. Enemy aeroplanes active.	
	27.1.17		General Machine Gun Training.	
	28.1.17		Church parade. Football match during afternoon. Improvements to camp. Enemy aircraft active.	
	29.1.17		General Machine Gun Training. Tactical scheme during afternoon. Enemy aircraft active.	
	30.1.17		Cleaning guns, ammunition & preparatory to moving up the line 1965 M.G. Coy.	
	31.1.17		Inspection of camp &c. Move to Canal Bank to relieve 196th M.G. Coy.	

D.O'Keefe
for O.C. 113th M.G. Coy
1.2.17

Army Form C. 2118.

WAR DIARY or INTELLIGENCE SUMMARY

(Erase heading not required.)

Instructions regarding War Diaries and Intelligence Summaries are contained in F. S. Regs, Part II. and the Staff Manual respectively. Title Pages will be prepared in manuscript.

No. 113 MACHINE GUN COY. 21 MAR 1917 MACHINE GUN CORPS.

Place	Date	Hour	Summary of Events and Information	Remarks and references to Appendices
YPRES SECTOR	31:1:17		Relieved 196th M.G.Coy in Centre Brigade. Relief complete by 9.25 P.M.	
	1:2:17		Very cold. Hard frost. Wind dangerous. Pte Hawes Leave to U.K.	
	2:2:17		Enemy bombardment on BOESINGHE SECTOR 5 A.M. We replied continually from 8 A.M to 4 P.M Enemy aeroplanes active. Our artillery shelled enemy front-line opposite Brigade on our right from 2 P.M to 4 P.M	
	3:2:17		Enemy aeroplanes active. Pte Jones H Leave to U.K. Intermittent shelling on both sides during the day.	
	4:2:17		Enemy Machine Guns active during the night. Enemy aeroplanes active	
	5:2:17		Bad visibility all day. R.Es Blowing up ice on CANAL north of YPRES SALIENT Very quiet.	
	6:2:17		Bad visibility all day. R.Es Blowing up ice on CANAL north of YPRES SALIENT Very quiet. Lt E.R.Robinson from Leave U.K. 70235 Pte HAWES R.W Died of Wounds 11868 L/Cpl CANNON W.H. Wounded 35818 Pte EUIOT R. from Leave U.K. 70226 Pte WHALL P.A Wounded	
	7:2:17		Practice shot took place at 9 P.M. on "S.O.S" Lines (M.Guns) 11868 L/Cpl CANNON W.H + 35818 Pte WHALL P.A. to 46 C.C.S suffering from wounds in waist and leg respectively. Col Intermittent shelling on both sides during the day 28186 Gr ELVIDGE C and 72668, Pte MORRIS J Leave to U.K.	
	8:2:17		Enemy aerial activity. A large sheet of flame observed behind Enemy Lines. Col Enemy Machine Guns active. Intermittent shelling during day. Col 2/Lt H.J TOBIN.	
	9:2:17		Reinforcement from Base arrived 10/2/17. 36497, Pte DAVIES A., 46507, Pte JONES E.H, 26701 Pte SHEPPARD G. Reinforcements from Base arrived 11/4/17	
	10/12/2/17		do	
	13:2:17	8.15 am	Enemy bombarded our front Line with H.E. Shells and Trench Mortars. We replied during afternoon.	
	14:2:17		Enemy aerial activity. Intermittent shelling during day. Hard frost.	
	15:2:17		Capt. C.B. HIBBERT, D.S.O. Leave to U.K. 4184 Pte LONG M.A Leave to U.K. Intermittent shelling during day	
	16:2:17		Heavy Enemy Bombardment at 1.30 am. Fire returned behind Enemy Lines at 6.15 PM (CAESARS NOSE) 9.	
	17:2:17		Enemy Aeroplanes active. Intermittent Shelling Cold. the enemy shelled German Defences 2 A.M	
	18:2:17		31908 Pte GRAY J., 62879, Pte DRIVER A. wounded by shell. shelter wounded German Trenches 3 AM. No.2 manned gun.	
	19/20/2/17		Intermittent Shelling during day, otherwise quiet. 2/Lt F.V.T. McDONALD Kingfisher to 107 M.G Coy	
	21/2/17		Active enemy bombardment on our Right. Dissimiled Front. 5-6 P.M. 16409 4Cpl SMITH B/H to L From Base 2/Lt M.R KING arrived Reinforcements from Base	
	22/23/24/17		Very quiet during day + night. Occasional amount of Enemy Machine Gun Fire during nights 23-24.2.17	
	25/2/17		Intermittent shelling during day. Enemy raided our Trenches 3 A.M all Machine Guns fired on S.O.S Lines 26979, Q/Cpl COUSEY H.L 9 wounded by hand grenade in mouth. Gun at C.14.2, shrapnel through Barrel casing, put of action. (Temporarily)	
	26/2/17		Two aeroplanes over our lines Enemy Machine Guns active.	
	27/2/17		Intermittent shelling during the night Enemy Machine Guns active. Intermittent shelling during day. Machine Gun at C.14.3	
	18/2/17		Fired 5 P.M. by TRENCH MORTAR	

D.A.Knight Major 113th M.G.Coy.

113th MACHINE GUN COMPANY Vol XI

WAR DIARY

FOR

MARCH 1917.

WAR DIARY
or
INTELLIGENCE SUMMARY

Army Form C. 2118.

(Erase heading not required.)

Instructions regarding War Diaries and Intelligence Summaries are contained in F.S. Regs., Part II. and the Staff Manual respectively. Title Pages will be prepared in manuscript.

No. 113 MACHINE GUN COY. 1917

Place	Date	Hour	Summary of Events and Information	Remarks and references to Appendices
YPRES SECTOR	1/3/17		Enemy motors active. 2/Lt Sketchley arrived from leave at Chateau Trois Tours.	
	2/3/17		Capt Crawford O.S.O. returned from leave to U.K. also Pte Long. Enemy registered morning try seems carried out.	
			LA FRAYE. 2000 Rnds fired indirect Fricka (Indirect).	
	3/3/17		3000 Rnds fired on enemy communication trenches.	
	4/3/17		Enemy aircraft active. 2 driven off by Anti-aircraft guns. Enemy trench mortar in Nun's Wood line. 2000 Rnds fired on enemy trenches.	
	5/3/17		Enemy T.M. very active on Canal Bank. 6,500 Rnds fired on S.O.S. line.	
	6/3/17		Enemy artillery active. Two retaliations fired.	
	7/3/17		Enemy shelled Eastern Bank nr MARENGO HSE. 3000 Rnds indirect fires on enemy trenches.	
	8/3/17		Enemy v. slow active down canal. 1000 Rnds indirect fired on Brompton Barks. Sgt Nutkin & Pte Perrin to 117th R. Gen. and appt. C.S.M. to that Coy.	
	9/3/17		Ditto, ditto. 7 Enemy aircraft. 1000 Rnds indirect	
	10/3/17		Enemy shells round in rear of canal. 3 section moved to Dorrin Dug-out. Morning. 7 Sections shelled in billets 2000 Rnds from own entrained T.Gns. two machine apparently damaged.	
	11/3/17		Hails accepted arrive. 2000 Rnds from own entrained T.Gns. two machine apparently damaged.	
	12/3/17		Returned to their own billets. H. Lyell to first German trench. Enc. to Base.	
	13/3/17		Enemy artillery active. 3600 Canal Bank. Our own v. active. 5000 Rnds fired on Brompton Bks during night.	
	14/3/17		Hostile aircraft over lines. Our artillery v. active. 2000 Rnds on enemy tramway. 2000 Rnds on enemy tramways. Pte Scott Special leave 6.U.K. 14/3/17 – 24/3/17.	
	15/3/17		Enemy shelled camel track. Hostile observation balloon up. 1000 Rnds fired on enemy tracks.	
	16/3/17		Enemy trenches & wire in rear.	
	17/3/17		2 Aeroplane Balloons approach carrying mail bags (Patrol) sent over enemy lines. Our aircraft active.	
	18/3/17		1300 Rounds fired on enemy trenches. Hostile O. Balloon up. S.O.S. allotter 2000 ammunition. Enemy was repulsed.	
	19/3/17		Enemy artillery active. 2/Lt Bullock moved to join the 3000 Rnd indirect firing day & night on Enemy trips. trip	
	20/3/17		S.A.M.L. Coy No. The Coy lose 2 Septm r.k.p. 2000 Rnds indirect moved to Toyes Dump. Right relieve Front lines 114 M.G. Coy.	

Army Form C. 2118.

WAR DIARY
or
INTELLIGENCE SUMMARY
(Erase heading not required.)

113 I.S. Coy
1917

Place	Date	Hour	Summary of Events and Information	Remarks and references to Appendices
YPRES SECTOR.	21.III.17 to 30/31.III.17		From 29/21.III.17 rearrangement of posters: the Right Brigade abandons LANCASHIRE Fm section. One half Coy remained in line in CENTRE AREA (area between SKIPTON ROAD & BOES:N GATE SECTOR): the other half Company going into training with the BRIGADE HQ BOIS 2EEBE Area.	
	21.III.17		Enemy reported during day and shelled batteries in rear. He raided Front line 2½.21-III.17 on 5000 rounds S.O.S. fired.	
	22.III.17		Very quiet day. occasional hostile shelling.	
	23.III.17		Hostile aircraft over the line. Enemy shelling on CANAL BANK and Farm behind.	
	24.III.17		Hostile aircraft very active. Artillery again active. 2 Enemy aircraft brought down near YPRES. 3000 rounds indirect fire on enemy communication trenches.	
	25.III.17 26.III.17		Occasional hostile enemy artillery. Our aircraft active.	
	27.III.17 28.III.17 29.III.17		Hostile artillery active. Artillery activity chiefly counter battery work.	
	30.III.17		Mutual artillery. Our heavy trench Mortars fired on BOESINE Front line on left. Quiet day. Normally. Day normal.	
	31/3/17		Raid in aft by Belgians caused exchange of shelling on our part + on enemy's. S.O.S. sent up at 1.15am. 3000 Rounds fired. Detachment from Skipton took up position in Lancs Farm SCOTT Enemy slipshod on entrenched between NILE & SKIPTON.	

E.H. Robertson Lt. I/C 113 I.S. Coy.

XI/96

113 MACHINE GUN COMPANY.

WAR DIARY

FOR

APRIL 1917

Army Form C. 2118.

WAR DIARY
or
INTELLIGENCE SUMMARY

(Erase heading not required.)

1/13th M G Coy

St JULIEN 1/10,000

Place	Date	Hour	Summary of Events and Information	Remarks and references to Appendices
YPRES SECTOR	1/4/17		Enemy aeroplane activity during day. Trench Mortar activity on BOESINGHE SECTOR about 10 A.M. Systematic registration by Enemy between NILE (C13 d 60 60) + SKIPTON (C14 c 40 20) Intermittent shelling on both sides during day.	
	2/4/17		" " Intermittent shelling on both sides during day.	
	3/4/17		" " Enemy artillery normal	
	4/4/17		Enemy machine Guns active during night. Enemy machine guns active during night. Enemy shells reported to have burst with double simultaneous sound. Believed new type of gas shell	
	5/4/17		Enemy aeroplanes active during day. Enemy aeroplanes active during afternoon. Enemy shelled LANCASHIRE FARM (C14.8.10.20) and HUDDERSFIELD ROAD (C13 d 60 30) during afternoon. Enemy 6" B wh from 12 Noon to 12.30 PM. Irregular M.G. Fire throughout night 3/4/17 Enemy shelled bridges 6.7 (C19 b 30 00) 6 B (C13 C 20 10) and 6 W. (C 13. C 30 20) about 11 PM. Enemy m. guns not so active. Heavy bombardment on extreme right between 9.30 PM and 10.15 P.M.	
	6/4/17		Enemy M Guns active during night - quiet during day.	
	7/4/17		Enemy aeroplane activity during early morning and afternoon. At 8 PM several aeroplanes took place to the night of YPRES. There were few explosions in all	
	8/4/17		One British aeroplane brought down East of PILCKEM ROAD at 4.30 PM (Approx C20 C Central)	
	9/4/17		Quiet day generally.	
	10/4/17		Artillery active on Right Brigade Front during day. Heavy bombardment of YPRES between 8-9 PM. Portion of CLOTH HALL TOWER knocked down. Aerial activity on both sides during afternoon. [Machine Gun Fire during night 10/11/4/17 Between 5-5.30 A.M. enemy sent up RED LIGHTS]	
	11/4/17		SOUTH OF YPRES. Enemy aeroplane activity during afternoon. Artillery on both sides quiet.	
	12/4/17		Bad visibility throughout day - artillery on both sides quiet.	
	13/4/17		Quiet day generally. Heavy bombardment on BOESINGHE SECTOR from 9.30 PM to 10.30 PM. All machine Gunners of all Unit ordered on their SOS lines	
	14/4/17		Quiet day generally. aeroplane activity on both sides during day.	
	15/4/17		do	

2449 Wt. W14957/M90 750,000 1/16 J.B.C. & A. Forms/C.2118/12.

Army Form C. 2118.

WAR DIARY
INTELLIGENCE SUMMARY

(Erase heading not required.)

113th M G Coy

ST JULIEN 1/10,000

Place	Date	Hour	Summary of Events and Information	Remarks and references to Appendices
YPRES SECTOR	16/4/17		Had machine guns active throughout day. Enemy machine guns active during night. Relieved by 114th Machine Gun Company, proceeding to "S" Camp (A 23. C. 50 80)	
	17/4/17		Proceeded to "H" Camp (A 10 a central) arriving there 12 Noon. Cleaning Guns &c.	
	18/4/17		Machine Gun Training	
	19/4/17		do and Bombing at "H" Camp. Revolver Competition held A 24 & 90.90. 1st and 2nd Prizes obtained by this unit	
	20/4/17		Machine Gun Training - Half-Company on Range (A 24 a 90 90) all day	
	21/4/17		Preparing for relief	
	22/4/17		Relieved 114 Machine Gun Company in LANCASHIRE FARM SECTOR	
	23/4/17		Enemy aeroplanes active during afternoon. Enemy machine guns active during night.	
	24/4/17		do	
	25/4/17		at 10 pm artillery on both sides opened fire - caused by bombing on Right Brigade Front - no raid took place.	
	26/4/17		Enemy Trench Mortared Front Line for 4-6 pm - we replied with Trench Mortars. Enemy Observation Balloon up in forenoon.	
	27/4/17		Enemy shelled our front line at irregular intervals during afternoon. Aerial activity on both sides throughout day.	
	28/4/17		Quiet day generally	
	29/4/17		From 10 am - 4 pm our artillery shelled enemy 1st and 2nd line. Trenches (C 14 a central) Aerial activity	
	30/4/17		Intermittent shelling on both sides during day. Intense bombardment and TRENCH MORTARS) on C.14 a and C 14 b Read by WELSH REGIMENT Artillery on both sides died down by 1.36 AM. opened By our artillery	

D O'Neill ft π.M.3rd M G Coy
1/5/16

Army Form C. 2118.

WAR DIARY
INTELLIGENCE SUMMARY
(Erase heading not required.)

113 M G Coy
Vol 13

Place	Date	Hour	Summary of Events and Information	Remarks and references to Appendices
YPRES	1/5/17		Artillery activity on both sides during day and night. Aerial activity on both sides during afternoon.	
SECTOR	2/5/17		do	
	3/5/17		Trench Mortar activity in BOESINGHE SECTOR during enemy's resting for 1 hour. Enemy aeroplane brought down at P/C ELVERDINGHE.	
	4/5/17		Quiet day generally. Gas alarm 11.20 p.m. Aerial activity on both sides.	
	5/5/17		Our heavy artillery shelled well behind enemy lines. Gas alarm 10.15 p.m.	
	6/5/17		Intermittent shelling on both sides throughout the day. Enemy aeroplanes active during afternoon.	
	7/5/17		Enemy plane over our lines at 2.30 p.m. flying low. Heavy shelling of YPRES from 7.45 p.m. onwards.	
	8/5/17		At 8.30 p.m. our artillery opened intense bombardment lasting 10 min. Enemy repeated lightly on Canal Bank. At 11 p.m. our artillery repeated - retaliation very weak.	
	9/5/17		Quiet day generally - no aerial activity on either side	
	10/5/17		Aerial activity on both sides - quiet during day generally.	
	11/5/17		Considerable aerial activity on both sides during day - slight shelling on both sides.	
	12/5/17		Heavy bombardment S of YPRES about 11 p.m.	
	13/5/17		Aerial activity on both sides during day. Quiet day generally.	
	14/5/17		At 3.8 a.m. enemy opened intense bombardment. We replied. Quiet day generally.	
	15/5/17		Quiet day generally. Usual aerial activity on both sides during the day.	
	16/5/17		do	
	17/5/17		Occasional counter battery work	
	18/5/17		Trench Mortar activity on left (BOESINGHE) during afternoon	
	19/5/17		Relieved by 114 MG Coy. marched to Y Camp - excellent billet outside HOUTKERQUE Foot inspection	
	20/5/17		marched to HOUTKERQUE - Bathing and running	
	21/5/17		Overhauling of Guns, ammunition etc. M.G. Training	
	22/5/17-25/5/17		M.G. Training and instruction on German Gun.	
	26/5/17		marched to A 14. & B 3 arriving 6.30 p.m. Capt C B HIBBERT, DSO and officers reconnoitring line	

2449 Wt. W14957/M90 750,000 1/16 J.B.C. & A. Forms/C.2118/12.

WAR DIARY or INTELLIGENCE SUMMARY

Army Form C. 2118.

Place	Date	Hour	Summary of Events and Information	Remarks and references to Appendices
YPRES SECTOR	27/5/17		Inspection and Church Parades.	
	28/5/17		2, 3 & 4 Sections constructed emplacements up the line, prior to shoot.	
	29/5/17		M G Training	
	30/5/17		At 6 p.m. 2, 3 & 4 Sections opened rapid fire on enemy trenches for 15 minutes, then returning to camp	
	31/5/17		M G Training in Camp A 14 B. S 3.	

J. Arnuh.
for O. 113 M.Y. Coy

13th MACHINE GUN COMPANY

WAR DIARY

FOR

JUNE 1917

WAR DIARY or INTELLIGENCE SUMMARY

Army Form C. 2118.

Place	Date	Hour	Summary of Events and Information	Remarks and references to Appendices
In the field	11.6.17	—	Artilling active on both sides — 10.40a-11.30p + 2.45p + 3.15a Aerial activity throughout day	
	12.6.17	—	Artillery very active at intervals during day. Enemy in of pot normal	
YPRES SALIENT	13.6.17	—	do — do — do — Enemy sun far too turbulent in BOESINGHE ARE in afternoon	
	14.6.17	—	Heavy counter battery work during day. Enemy aerial activity during afternoon evening	
	15.6.17	—	Enemy artillery very active my trafs S, 6.13.6.b ? Communication trenches in Section Aerial activity on both sides	
	16.6.17	—	Artillery active in Art sector (Area Shooting) Corps Artillery work	
			11.6.17. R.G. Corps wireless C.14.1, C.14.2, C.14.3, C.19.1, C.10.1, boundary	
	17.6.17	—	Heavy hostile shelling between 9-11 pm on trenches & bridges. FARGATE STRONG POINT	
	18.6.17	—	Trench mortar activity in BOESIN in 6.115 SECTOR hostile artillery fire (inaction) Aerial activity on both sides	
	19.6.17	—	Occasional light shelling for hrs. Enemy shelling last 24 hours in ESSEX CORNER + BRIDGE S.	
	20.6.17	—	Enemy trolley work all day - Aerial activity on both sides during afternoon ? Enemy	
	21.6.17	—	Aerial activity during day Artillery fire on both sides. In of his aeroplane	
	22.6.17	—	Enemy artillery shelling trench area aerial forenoon + afternoon aerial activity	
	23.6.17	—	Enemy artillery active in mop + trefl railways. Very little hostile aerial activity aeroplane	
	24.6.17	—	Heavy hostile shelling during day memory in intensity at dusk — do —	
	25.6.17	—	do — — Aerial activity during afternoon.	
	26.6.17	—	Enemy shelled CANAL BANK + bridges during day	
	27.6.17	—	do — do —	
	28.6.17	—	Enemy trench anno 2f m 0.13 also ? Jem aeroplanes (Scout) Enemy artillery active.	
	29.6.17	—	Relieved by 87th tus G. Coy. Back for Summer Training at APPSMORT.	
	30.6.17	—	From 11.6.17 to 26.6.17 this unit has fired 217,803 rds on Enemy Communication trenches, roads, & light railways.	

W. Prevost
Lt 113 M.G. Coy

MC #515

113 Machine Gun Company

War Diary

July 1-1917

WAR DIARY
or
INTELLIGENCE SUMMARY

Army Form C. 2118.

113th M.G. Coy

Place	Date	Hour	Summary of Events and Information	Remarks and references to Appendices
Ypres	1st July		M.G. Training for the Offensive at Pipemont.	
	15 July		Move by bus to CAESTRE AREA	
	15 "		" " " PROVEN AREA	
	16 "		" " "	
	17 "		" " "	
	18 "		M.G. Training	
	19/20 "		Coy relieve 87th M.G. Coy in ZWAANHOF SECTOR Y Line (A.14 & B.8)	
	21 "		Transport moved to Brigade Transport Lines. Considerable artillery activity on both sides. Aerial activity on both sides	
	22 "		Hostile artillery activity. Gas shells being employed. " " " "	
	23 "		" " " " " " " "	
	24 "		" " " Enemy M.G's active	
	25 "		15th Bn. K.L.F. relieve enemy trenches (C.7.c.60.70 & Jessie 28.N.W.2) 7.30 to 10 am the Brunswickers	
	26 "		Hostile artillery active on back areas. Communication trenches & dugouts	
	27 "		Gas shelling of front line	
	28 "		2nd line recipient trenches during "relief"	
	29 "		Artillery both sides very active. Lively battery work during afternoon	
	30 "		An artillery very active – Enemy batteries fairly back	
	31 "		Z Day	N. Watson Lt for O 113 M.G. Coy

Vol 16

113th Machine Gun Company

113/38

War Diary

August 1917

WAR DIARY or INTELLIGENCE SUMMARY

Army Form C. 2118.

(Erase heading not required.)

Place	Date	Hour	Summary of Events and Information	Remarks and references to Appendices
PILCKEM + LANGEMARCK RIDGE	August 1/4		Brief Summary of the operations between July 31st + the night of August 4/5 is attached. The Casualties during these operations amounted to 1 Officer wounded; 3 OR killed and 24 OR wounded.	
	5		Entrained ELVERDINGHE for PROVEN. Marched billets at WORMHOUDT.	
	6		Gay spent drawing up Programmes.	
	7/17		A programme of Training was arranged, to put through 4 hours a day (after 2½ hours daily Physical Training) attention being paid to Musketry, drill, Musketry.	
	18		Returned to line relieving 20th Division in LANGEMARCK Sector. This Company was ordered to take up 12 positions N of the STEENBEEK, + form an SOS Battery. One Section in reserve. Came under very heavy shelling on our Journey to our Tanks. Nothing particular to report in spite of over very heavy shelling our positions were Taranbless.	
	19/27			
	28		115 Brigade attacked on their front, our Reserve Section was brought into action for Barrage fire. We were heavily shelled + after firing for 1½ hours 4 guns + 3 Withdrew 115 th on the 4 in LANGEMARCK + gun Cage. Battery Guns Subalterns Capt Artillery gunfire Captain from 148 Bn 7 died of severe wounds attached main from 148 Bn 7 by Antly	

Ref: MESSAGE PAD
D.1.   OPERATIONS DURING PERIOD 31 JULY to 4 AUGUST 1917

The 113th M.G. Coy acted under instructions as follows:-

No 1st Section under direct command of the D.M.G.O. Ten minutes after ZERO No 1 Section proceeded to MAUSER COT where from +1.15 to +3.45 they put a barrage along line C.3.A.80.60. to C.3.B.30.50. C.3.B.50.50. to C.3.B.75.75 approx. After this they rejoined H.Q. at FARGATE STRONG POINT.

No 2 Section. Two Guns proceeded to HOUSE 10 and ZOUAVE HOUSE respectively. The ZOUAVE HOUSE GUN arrived before the Infantry and fired 750 Rounds direct at running targets. A few Germans were seen to fall.
Other two Guns of this Section were in Brigade Reserve at FARGATE STRONG POINT.

No 4 Section   Two Guns proceeded to TELEGRAPH HOUSE and CHIMNEY HOUSE respectively: other two proceeded to SAPEUR HOUSE and to a S.P. about C.2.d.0.6.
These three sections followed the Infantry as closely as possible and successfully crossed the GERMAN FRONT LINE before any definite barrage came down. No 1 Section rejoined at FARGATE H.Q. at ZERO +5 hours without having sustained a single casualty.

No 3 Section   Original instructions could not exactly be carried out for the Infantry dug in primarily, just behind road running N.W from IRON CROSS. Guns of the Section took up positions along this line and helped to reduce S.P. at NORMAN JUNCTION where some 30 GERMANS surrendered and 4 Machine Guns were captured.
On the following day, 1st AUGUST, the 115 M.G. Coy were relieved by this Coy and the dispositions were as follows:-

Nos 4 & 2 Sections moved to STRAY FARM; their duty being to put barrage fire along line parallel with BRIGADE FRONT (which was from the BOESINGHE-THOUROUT RLY to THE INGS inclusive). This barrage line was 600 yards East of the R. STEENBEEK.

No I. moved to points U.28.C.05.06, U.27.C.75.65, U.27.C.44 and U.27.C.80.35. and NO III moved into reserve at FARGATE SP.
On the 3rd AUGUST NO III relieved No I in forward positions.
On the 4th AUGUST the 12 Guns in the Line were relieved by the 114 M.G. Coy and No 1 Section moved up to our original positions in and behind BLACK LINE, being attached temporarily to 115 Infy Bgde.
This Section moved out the following evening, 5/6 AUGUST and rejoined Company on the 6th AUGUST.

The Transport arrangements could not be followed to the letter owing to the mud. Auxiliary dump was made at BOCHE HOUSE, a central spot, comparatively, for all ration parties. Rations were through every day and no team was without food during the whole period of operations.

                                                           B. Abbott Capt.
10th AUGUST, 1917   O.C. 113 M.G. Coy.

113th Machine Gun Company.
Vol 17

War Diary
for
September 1917.

WAR DIARY
or
INTELLIGENCE SUMMARY.
(Erase heading not required.)

Army Form C. 2118.

Place	Date	Hour	Summary of Events and Information	Remarks and references to Appendices
YPRES - Salient	1917 -4/9/17		Company are in the line at Langemark. No casualties.	Saston
(MALAKOFF) Farm	5th		Company plan on section drove relieved & returning to MALAKOFF Farm area. No casualties.	
	6-9th		Left in the line on Anti-aircraft work. Reorganisation and M.G. training. Malakoff Farm area. On the 8th the G.O.C. NShf. Bde presents holiday awards. Nofollowing are awarded to this unit. Military Medal 11205 Sgt. L.North, 11855 Sgt Fleming R, 26988 Cpl Johnson P., 84493 Pte Pearce T, (42285 Sgt Brotznjeola service certificate 11205 Sgt Nott L. 10079 Sgt Farke. Ren. W. not present receive medal) 26988 Cpl Anna W, 33276(?) Cpl Evant B. 26707 Cheleton R. 11862 Cheleton R. 14994 Sgt Myles. 4784 Mallary No, 23690 Pte Bradstreet h.	
PROVEN 2.H.9.J	9th	13th	Entrained at ELVERDINGHE for PROVEN Area. M.G. Drawing in St Area. This comprises chiefly Route marches, drill, handling orders.	
	9-15th		8-10 mile daily. Brigade Route March - Moved to Ecke Area. } During the four days no men fell " HAZEBROUCK " } out on the line of march. " ESTAIRES " " ERQUINGHEM - LYS.	
H3 & H4 BELGIUM 7 Parts FRANCE 7 Sheet 36	17th 20th		Relieve 17th MG Coy in Bois GRENIER SECTION. During last fortnight the area has been quiet. Our activity between Night firing (8000 per night) and anti-aircraft work. Chiefly engaged in constructional work.	
	30			

W.Wright
Ajk 113 MGC

113TH MACHINE GUN COMPANY. Vol 18

WAR DIARY.

FOR

OCTOBER 1917.

Army Form C. 2118.

No. 113
MACHINE GUN COMPANY.

No. ....
Date 1/11/17

WAR DIARY
or
INTELLIGENCE SUMMARY

(Erase heading not required.)

Instructions regarding War Diaries and Intelligence Summaries are contained in F.S. Regs., Part II. and the Staff Manual respectively. Title Pages will be prepared in manuscript.

Place	Date	Hour	Summary of Events and Information	Remarks and references to Appendices
BOIS GRENIER SECTION	1/10/17		Artillery TMs & machine guns on both sides quiet, Enemy aircraft over our gun position T.15 a 05.4.1 at 1AM & fired about 100 rounds at Gun team	
	2/10/17		Enemy artillery slightly more active, TM's on either side normal	
	3/10/17		Artillery & M.G's normal	
	4/10/17		Enemy artillery slightly more active, M.G's on either side normal	
	5/10/17		Everything normal except enemy TMs which were slightly more active	
	6/10/17		Everything normal, a faid gtl firing at frequent intervals over LONDON BRIDGE from INCOMPLETE TRENCH or INCOMPLETE SUPPORT	
	7/10/17		Everything normal except enemy aircraft which were slightly more active	
	8/10/17		Gun at T.19 fired 750 rounds on S.O.S. lines at 1 A.M.	
	9/10/17		Artillery on either side slightly more active, Enemy planes more active, German flares over lines at 4.30 PM fired at by our M.G's & appeared to fall in the direction of WEZ MACQUART	
	10/10/17		Artillery on either side more active, Aircraft fairly active, we fired 5000 rounds on enemy planes, Sound like STROMBOS HORNS heard in enemy line run WEZ MACQUART at 6.45 PM - lasted 1 min	
	11/10/17		Everything normal	
	12/9/17		Artillery both sides fairly active, Enemy TMs very active 5.50 – 6.15 PM on our front line, Gun M.G's (9) fired 4000 rounds on SOS lines at 5.50 A.M.	
	13/10/17		Everything normal	
	14/10/17		do We fired slightly more in A/A work than usual	
	15/10/17		Very quiet	
	16/10/17		Slightly increased activity all round, Enemy shelled PR13 POT particularly	

Army Form C. 2118.

WAR DIARY
or
INTELLIGENCE SUMMARY
(Erase heading not required.)

No. 113 MACHINE GUN COMPANY.
No. ....
Date 1/11/17

Instructions regarding War Diaries and Intelligence Summaries are contained in F. S. Regs., Part II. and the Staff Manual respectively. Title Pages will be prepared in manuscript.

Place	Date	Hour	Summary of Events and Information	Remarks and references to Appendices
BOIS GRENIER SECTION	17/10/17		do	
	18/10/17		Everything normal except enemy aircraft which were slightly more active	
	19/10/17		Everything normal	
	20/10/17		Enemy artillery slightly more active	
	21/10/17		Everything normal	
	22/10/17		do do	
	23/10/17		Very quiet	
	24/10/17		do do	
	25/10/17		Enemy aircraft active. We fired some 1000 rounds A/A work	
	26/10/17		Quiet	
	27/10/17		Quiet except for enemy T.M's which fired on our front line from 12.45 to 1.15 PM during day. Everything quiet except enemy planes at which we fired some 4,500 rounds. 9.30 PM to 10 PM six of our guns co-operated with artillery etc in gas bombardment. These guns were at I.20.c.88.59 I.19.D.50.79 I.9.c.3.1 I.15.a.05.45 I.25.B.35.65 I.25.c.65.45 14,000 rounds were fired	
	28/10/17			
	29/31/17		Everything normal	

K.B. Hyall Lt
for 2/0c 113 M.G. Coy.

No 19

115 MACHINE GUN COMPANY

WAR DIARY

FOR

NOVEMBER 1917

Army Form C. 2118.

WAR DIARY
or
INTELLIGENCE SUMMARY.
(Erase heading not required.)

No. 118 MACHINE GUN COMPANY.
No. ....
Date 1.12.17

Place	Date	Hour	Summary of Events and Information	Remarks and references to Appendices
POS S GRENIER SECTOR	1.11.17 31.11.17		The past month has been a matter of holding the line in defensive S.O.S. positions. By night and day the guns have been: S.O.S shoots, retaliation shoots, covering fire for Trench Mortar (Heavy) and harassing fire on Relief Routes, Ramming etc. Also A-A work.	
	4/5th	1.a.m 1.30	Enemy Gas-shelled Support and Subsidiary lines. No Casualties. Harassing was found effective for the Enemy Parries on two searchlights and four Enemy machine guns opened spasmodic fire.	
	5/6th 7th		Flank M.G.s cooperated in conjunction with Operation of Left Brigade, Infantry raid Bangalore torpedoes in confunction with Operation of Inch Trench 116d 50.90. and another party silenced Enemy machine at 122a 26.53. N. 93 fires in Cooperation on 122a 80.10; 122a 80.30; 122a 75.09.; 122a 20.10.; 127 + 30.20 and 127 + 30.90. Rapid fire for 15 minutes. 1500 Rnds per Gun. No Identification obtained. No M.G. Casualties.	
	12/13th 6.30 to 7.30 p.m		Enemy projected gas from INCIDENT SUPPORT I16a. No M.G Casualties.	
	13/14th 10.15 p.m		Enemy shelled front Support together half an hour and repeated between 11 to 11.20 p.m. Guns opened on S.O.S. lines. No Infantry action took place apparently. Enemy harassed S.A. on Sand bag line and C.T's.	
	29/19th 11.15 p.m		Enemy heart went out of PATRICK Post 126a 70.65. 15 Enemy were seen crawling towards outlines. Guns opened on S.O.S. lines. Enemy retired. None found by Wire patrol etc. No M.G Casualties.	

No. 1 Reports S.A.A. consumed in harassing fire etc during the month: 14,600

[Signature] Capt Mon ?
O.C M.G.

113th MACHINE GUN COY
Vol 20

WAR DIARY
FOR
DECEMBER 1917.

WAR DIARY or INTELLIGENCE SUMMARY

Army Form C. 2118.

Place	Date	Hour	Summary of Events and Information	Remarks and references to Appendices
BOIS GRENIER SECTOR	1·XII·17		Quiet day. Enemy fire shelled back areas.	
Sheet 36 NW 4 & 6 1/20,000	2·XII·17 5th 6 1/20,000		Very quiet. Enemy in retaliation. Enemy attempts to book on zero fire RH 12·O·a. Moved the position by S.O.S. Enemy aircraft active. Enemy aircraft flew over fire line constantly every night with Gipo on Enemy wires which have been cut by generally with machine gun fire. Shelled our artillery vij. INCH TRENCH 116.b.70.05 to 116.b.55.00 and 116.d.50.73 and INCREASE TRENCH I.31.d.50.50 to I.31.d.85.60. This machine in preparation for probable raids & to carried out.	
Trench Belgium sheet 36	20·K		The 10th Australian Infy Bde released fire great positions taking over ground between LEITH WALK inclusive to PARK ROW AVENUE exclusive, i.e. squares I.20a, 114d, 114b, I.15, I.16c and I.9c and D. Garrisons relieved returned to HQ. for night.	
Reserve maps	21·00		Garrisons relieved one Bn took over positions in areas vacated by the 114 Infy Bde during the same between PARK ROW AVENUE (apt. Road running SE) Sent out our new frontage lay between ELBOW FARM I.29.c.05.25 to N.6.a.4.0 through (I 20) to TIN BARN TRAMWAY H.50·1.9 Boys again map 36 N.W.4 to H.21 d. 4.5 (NEW FARM); Coy Headquarters moved from Arm-left Sector HQ was then at 119 c 9.5. Telephone France & Belgium map 36. Right Sector at I.25·c·3.3 and Right start I.36·a·3.1. Centre at CULVERT FARM I.25·c·3.3 and centre at Conl HQrs. Communication in attainable to Sec. from about I.28 Central. About 20 shells but Seastine, 5 Guns Enemy active between I·17 20th my gun was in submission lines, Each having its own machine gun Enemy aircraft details for Retaliation Shooting in addition.	
	23·00		were specially detailed for Retaliation Shooting in addition to our retaliation fire in vicinity of the twelve rifles detailed for AA & twist in my Battalion Bn dumps. Seven positions of the twelve were actually dumps. Tramways by day. Between 8th & 14th Decr. we put a Gun in N·M·L. covered by work. Between 8th & Rifleman at to commit a raid, which if successful states was likely above gun & party of Rifleman at to commit a raid, which (they) Stato were above about 500 yards take place. On the 12th there was an attempt about 500 yards N.W. of this spot.	

A5834. Wt. W4973/M687. 750,000. 8/16. D.D. & L. Ltd. Forms/C.2118/13.

Army Form C. 2118.

WAR DIARY
or
INTELLIGENCE SUMMARY.
(Erase heading not required.)

Instructions regarding War Diaries and Intelligence Summaries are contained in F. S. Regs., Part II. and the Staff Manual respectively. Title pages will be prepared in manuscript.

Place	Date	Hour	Summary of Events and Information	Remarks and references to Appendices
BOIS GRENIER & FLEURBAIX			General Principle. On taking over the new plan of ground we find the position was in the support line as STOPPING GUNS. his taking to cover gap between the Posts in close order like this (4000 yard frontage) the Battern my plan, it is thought, is the only practical system. Guns laid in parallel lines. Your communication with Bn headquarters could then be concentrated to cover the in Posts.	Gilbert Egerton Montague /

A.5834 Wt.W4973/M687 750,000 8/16 D.D.& L. Ltd. Forms/C.2118/13.

113th MACHINE GUN COY. Vol 21
WAR DIARY.
FOR
JANUARY 1918.

Army Form C. 2118.

References: 1/10,000 BELGIUM & FRANCE
BOIS GRENIER, RADINGHEM. Sheet 36. 1/40,000
36 SW2. BETHUNE
N.W. France
36 A 1:40,000

113 Machine Gun Company

WAR DIARY or INTELLIGENCE SUMMARY.
(Erase heading not required.)

Instructions regarding War Diaries and Intelligence Summaries are contained in F. S. Regs., Part II. and the Staff Manual respectively. Title pages will be prepared in manuscript.

Place	Date	Hour	Summary of Events and Information	Remarks and references to Appendices
Lewisbrad	Jan 1-13		Holding the line from PARK ROW AVENUE & TIN BARN AVENUE. Normal trench warfare during whole period. No raids attempted by either side. Three of our guns fired each night on hostile dumps, tracks and tramways. In all 48,000 rounds (indirect) were fired.	
BAC S¹ MAUR	Jan 14		On the night 13/14 Unit was relieved by 37th M. Coy. Company moved to billets at Rue S¹ Maur G-12 Belgian France map.	
	Jan 15		Coy moved to billets between Merville & Estaires L 20 d 50,60 France 36 A.	
	16-30		Training in General Gun work, Cloudorss drees, and Barrage Drill.	
	31st		Coy moved to GUARBECQUE, en route for SPECIAL MANOEUVRE AREA.	

Wright
for O.C. 113th M.G. Coy.

No. 113
MACHINE GUN
COMPANY.
No......
Date 2/2/18

Ya 22

War Diary
113. Machine Gun Company
February 1918

Ref: First Army
36 NW

WAR DIARY
or
INTELLIGENCE SUMMARY.
(Erase heading not required.)

Army Form C. 2118.

MACHINE GUN COMPANY.
No. W 113
Date 1/3/16

Place	Date	Hour	Summary of Events and Information	Remarks and references to Appendices
ENQUINEGATTE	1-11 incl		Company were out of line training in Steenvoorde Manoeuvre Area (1st Army) General programme Range Works Bomb Drill Barrage firing	
GUARBECQUE	12		Marched to GUARBECQUE - Stayed for night	
NEUF BERQUIN	13		" " NEUF BERQUIN " " "	
ARMENTIERES	14/23		Marched to ARMENTIERES - Took over from 172 M.G.Coy in ARMENTIERES SECTION. DISTRIBUTION, 2 Guns in Support, 6 Guns Subsidiary Line. 4 Guns Ferme de Jardins Line; 4 Guns under D.M.G.O. in Reserve. The 2 Guns in Support were in exposed positions but not altered on account of possibility of hostile raid on our front. Party of 2 officers 60 OR Germans raided 2 posts in Front Line, I.5.2 and I.5.3 and 2 posts behind in support line. Casualties in these posts slight. 2 German prisoners taken (1 died later) M Guns fired on SOS lines and each Gun in Support Line fired 1000 Rounds on the evacuated posts (1+2) which they were covering.	
	24/25		Capt. C.A.M. JACKSON resumed Command of Coy, vice Capt C.B.HIBBERT, D.S.O. attentat 2 i/c 18 Battn M.G Corps	
	27		During the period in line, 3 Guns per night have fired upon roads, tracks, new work in enemys lines. Ammunition expended 47,100 ROUNDS, S.A.A	
			Chief localities shelled by enemy during period 14-28 Feb: NOUVEL HOUPLINES, L.T.C. and vicinity of the DISTILLERY & Fme de la BUTERNE I.4.a.59 + B.28.c.7.3 Battle Casualties. 14/28 Feby. — 1	

R.B. White
2/Lt
for OC 113 M.G Coy

www.ingramcontent.com/pod-product-compliance
Lightning Source LLC
Chambersburg PA
CBHW081239170426
43191CB00034B/1987